Salt Lick Cookbook

★ ★ ★

A Story of Land, Family, and Love

SCOTT ROBERTS *&* JESSICA DUPUY

FOREWORD BY ADAM RICHMAN
PHOTOGRAPHY BY KENNY BRAUN

PHOTO AND ILLUSTRATION CREDITS

ALL PHOTOGRAPHY BY KENNY BRAUN

with the exception of
pages 253 and 255, photographers unknown

Food Styling by Meghan Erwin
Illustrations by Andy Dearwater
Copyediting by Dana Frank

THE SALT LICK PRESS
P.O. Box 311
Driftwood, TX 78619

Library of Congress Control Number: 2012938809

All rights reserved
Printed in China through Asia Pacific Offset
First Edition, 2012

Book and jacket design by
Julie Savasky and DJ Stout
Pentagram Design, Austin, Texas

This book is dedicated to strong Texas women

MAMMIE, ROXIE, HISAKO, SUSAN, AND MAILE.

Not because it's a cookbook, but because without strong

women like them, there would be no Texas.

CONTENTS

★ ★ ★

Foreword

HILL COUNTRY BARBECUE—like Bowie's knife, Crockett's hat, the Lone Star, J. R. Ewing, and a landscape dotted with oil derricks—is a widely accepted part of Texas lore. So it follows that when the owner of an iconic establishment for Hill Country barbecue writes a tome, collecting all its vast knowledge and history, he would ask a Jewish guy from Brooklyn to write the foreword.

Kidding aside, that is kind of the point. The Salt Lick restaurant, in all its glory, is so far from my world yet somehow immediately accessible. I have no touchstone for that kind of culinary craft in my own life. But from the moment I sampled its food, looked at the sprawling grounds, and took in the amazing Hill Country itself, I was filled with wonder and a sense of home.

That is due in no small part to owner Scott Roberts' vast culinary expertise and also to the environment he works in. Once you hear the engaging stories about the restaurant's conception—like Scott's father deciding where he wanted the pit by marking the spot in the ground with his boot, and Scott and his relatives actually constructing it—you know there is real history and legend in every bite. I could rhapsodize for hours about my first glimpse of the open pit at the Salt Lick. There are, of course, the succulent hanging sausages, the remarkable ribs, the near life-changing turkey (an anomaly at most barbecue establishments), and, naturally, the crown jewel of Texas barbecue, beef brisket.

Jews don't bring all that much to the lexicon of cooked meat. But Grandma's and Mom's brisket is the stuff of legend on the lips of every good Jewish boy. Every good Jewish boy thinks his grandma's or his mom's brisket is the best. And up until my first bite of the Salt Lick's brisket, I, too, was a good Jewish boy. But one bite of the pecan-smoked, oak-fired, spice-rubbed brisket from Driftwood, Texas, had me questioning both faith and family. Both taste buds and allegiances.

As lofty as that sounds, the greatness of the Salt Lick's menu cannot be overstated. The experience of going to the Salt Lick is absolutely transporting. The food is truly one-of-a-kind, and I never have had its equal. It is the apex of culinary skill plus personal history plus great ingredients. It's a story told in every laugh shared at the restaurant, in every "ooh," "aah," and "mmm," in every look of wonder as people stroll the grounds of vineyards, low-lying brambles and bushes, and decades upon decades of history. The story owes as much to Japan as it does to Lockhart and is as much about live oak as it is about quite possibly the best habanero sauce ever.

There is no place in the world like the Salt Lick, and there is no food in the world like the Salt Lick serves. It is with great pride that I am part of this book, of Scott and his team's giving you the keys to the kingdom, opening up a world of tradition and excellence, history and flavor. I am a better food TV personality for having eaten there and a more educated and appreciative eater.

Scott Roberts knows the story of where he's from and the story of Texas barbecue, and he knows the Salt Lick's place within that. You'll find more than just recipes in this book, certainly more than just the tale of one establishment. It is truly the tale of what an iconic food from an iconic place can be. And without question, it is a story worth reading and learning from. The food is out there, the flavor is out there—all you have to do is turn the page.

With joy and with respect—and looking forward to my next burnt end.

ADAM RICHMAN
Author, *America the Edible*
Host and Executive Producer, *Man v. Food Nation, Adam Richman's Best Sandwich in America*

Introduction

THE ROAD TO great barbecue is a journey. It is a quest that leads away from the bright lights and congested streets of the city, down winding roads, to places where life slows down, where the world feels peaceful and the destination is simply barbecue. Across Texas, such famed spots as Lockhart, Llano, Taylor, and Driftwood hold that distinction. Perhaps it's because great barbecue in itself requires a slow, peaceful process, one that begins and ends with a long-burning fire and a lot of patience.

The road to the Salt Lick, Driftwood's long-standing barbecue icon, winds west from Austin, through the Texas Hill Country. It's a narrow two-lane road that bends around ranches and homesteads and landscapes of live oak mots and cedar-post fences.

Drive with the windows down as you near the celebrated restaurant. The air becomes fragrant with smoke from the open pits, and it will guide you to an old wooden sign and the gravel parking lot. Now you can even close your eyes and follow the aroma to the rustic timber-and-limestone building. When you step in, the wooden screen door closes behind you and the world outside dissolves. All you see is the round open pit, layered with glistening brisket, sausage, and ribs, sizzling from a continuous live oak fire beneath and baking in the thick, flavorful smoke that rises into the wide smoke stack above. You have arrived.

In Texas and throughout the South, myriad barbecue joints claim the title of Best Barbecue. Many barbecue enthusiasts would nearly fight to the death to defend their favorite contender, and the Salt Lick is certainly one. But Salt Lick owner Scott Roberts doesn't care about that. He's more interested in the smiles on his customers' faces as they leave the restaurant. With more than 600,000 customers served each year, he may be on to something.

That's because Roberts is building on the foundation his family laid down more than 130 years ago, as his great grandparents made their long journey to Texas. On the trail, they prepared food and cooked meat in ways that preserved it. Roberts keeps those techniques because they are simple and proven. His great grandparents settled in Driftwood in the 1870s, and his grandparents farmed the land and were sustained by its bounty. They helped raise Roberts and instilled in him a love of the land. In 1967, Roberts' parents created an open pit barbecue stand that evolved into the Salt Lick of today. Roberts continues the journey into the Salt Lick's future.

This is not a book just about Salt Lick barbecue. It's about how the barbecue came to be: a story of respect for the land, its history, and the family that planted its roots in Driftwood and cultivated a well-deserved reputation. As Scott Roberts reveals in the following pages, this book is about a family's love for its home and the great food that comes out of that.

This is the story of the Salt Lick.

JESSICA DUPUY

CHAPTER ONE

DRIFTWOOD
A FAMILY HISTORY

★ ★ ★

WHAT DOES IT TAKE to make a great dish? Many might say the secret is in the ingredients, the technique, or a heralded recipe passed on from generation to generation. Those elements are all important. But the true answer is in the land and the people who care for it. It's the land that inspires the people. That's what my family taught me while growing up on our acreage in Driftwood. In the center of the land is a family restaurant, recognized more for its food—juicy brisket and ribs, fresh potato salad and coleslaw, signature barbecue sauce made from a century-old secret recipe, and peach cobbler that will send your eyes rolling to the back of your head—than for the story behind the food.

The restaurant is the Salt Lick. And though it's certainly a place that reveals a story about great Texas barbecue, it's really more about a love affair. If it weren't for my family's love for Driftwood, it would never have existed.

The roots of the Salt Lick restaurant run deep, but they didn't begin in Texas. They began in North Carolina in 1847, with the birth of my great grandfather, James A. Howard. He

Bettie "Mammie" Howard, with grand-daughter Nana V. Howard, ca. 1895.

served a brief time in the Confederate War and ended up as a surveyor in Desoto, Miss., long before the original open pit was ever built in Driftwood. In October 1874 Howard married a young but determined 20-year-old orphan, Sarah Madora Mitchel, whom most people called Bettie. (Most of the family called her Mammie.) She told him that she couldn't promise to ever love him, but that if he would marry her and take her to Texas, she would raise his kids and be good to him. Howard took her up on it. Within a week of their wedding day, the two left a land that they loved in search of a place they could love even more.

They weren't alone. After the Civil War, a wave of Southerners from the Carolinas, Georgia, and Mississippi headed for the wild frontier of Texas. James and Bettie joined friends John A. Garrison and his wife and two sons, as well as Bettie's brother John, on November 2, 1874, on a boat across the Gulf from Biloxi to Indianola, Texas. From there, they spent a few days assembling a wagon before heading west to find a place to settle.

Together they began a journey that would spark a family tradition and love for the land passed on through stories, family recipes, and the countless plates served at the Salt Lick restaurant today.

❧ TRAIL COOKING ❧

ALONG THE WAY, James and Bettie camped beneath the stars and cooked meals based on what little supplies and natural resources they had. Texas was largely unsettled at the time. Fresh water and outposts for garden-fresh produce were few and far between, leaving the best options for food in potatoes, onions, cabbage, vinegar, and spices, all of which kept longer than most other vegetables. The quick and easy cabbage salad, or slaw with vinegar and spices, as well as the warm potato salad mixed with onion, salt, pepper, and vinegar were simple, flavorful, and sustainable for the settlers. The recipes my family used then have been preserved for generations and are virtually the same that we serve at the Salt Lick today. There was no mayonnaise; there was no celery or pimento. They used what would last and kept recipes simple.

For meat, they hunted along the way or cooked beef they would buy at market. Cooking over an open campfire wasn't always easy, and there was little time and few resources to brine or marinate meat to tenderize it. They relied on an age-old method of cooking developed by Native Americans. "Earth berm," "earth hearth," "burned-rock middens," and "pit cooking" all refer to the method of cooking slowly over indirect heat to tenderize, cure, and flavor meat. The method included seasoning and then searing meat on an open flame to seal in the juices. Oftentimes the cooks would use a metal grate that they carried in the wagon as a grill surface held up by small makeshift rock walls. If the wind was blowing wrong, they would build an earth berm to hold in the heat and smoke. They could keep the fire going while moving hot coals to one side of the grate. The meats were set along the wall of the pit and left to cook for an extended period of time. As the settlers moved throughout Texas, they used different woods available along the way. Eventually, they began using live oak, which ultimately became their wood of choice for its density and smoke flavor.

That is how much of Texas barbecue originated. Though indigenous people around the world have used similar methods for cooking, barbecue as we know it in Texas is a conglomeration of Native American berm cooking from the Northeastern coast all along the Southern barbecue belt into Texas. Mexican vaquero cooking, richly influenced by bolder spices, was brought to Texas with the onset of Spanish exploration and later cattle ranching. To this day, the Salt Lick relies on the same open pit method used by its original settlers in conjunction with the modern and more commonly used cast-iron pits. We still feel the open pit is more traditional. As my father would say, "There weren't any bumper hitches on the wagons to haul around closed smoker pits." Our barbecue and the sides we serve reflect the methods and resources my great grand-parents used on their journey to Driftwood. As you'll soon find, the legacy of their journey to this part of Texas is revealed every day at the Salt Lick restaurant.

Example of how settlers would dig into the ground to create barbecue pits as they were traveling west toward Texas.

☙ DISCOVERING DRIFTWOOD ❧

Though hundreds of families had made the long journey before my great grand-parents, they still encountered hardships along the way. Often wagoners would band together to make the trip, but the Howards and Garrisons made the trip as a two-wagon party. Howard later relayed to his children after many years that they were often fearful along the way and that he and Garrison took turns guarding the wagons at night.

After five weeks on the trail from Indianola, James and Bettie Howard stopped to survey the Dallas area, but the prairies didn't suit them. I've often thought that had they stayed there, our family might own half of Dallas, but it wasn't in the cards.

They arrived in Martindale on December 14, 1874, and by the turn of the year, both families had rented farms in the area. Howard's farm was on the San Marcos River, where Bettie gave birth to their three sons, Edgar (1875), Christopher "Lum" Columbus (1877), and James Iverson (1879). But the Howards wanted to own land. Bettie was not fond of their location along the San Marcos River, because the mosquitoes were bad and the children often had chills and fever in the summer.

Howard eventually found some land on the south banks of the Colorado River in Austin that was for sale for 50 cents an acre—the land that is now home to Austin's famed Zilker Park. But where Zilker Park may be a prime plot of land for the Capital City today, it was smack dab in the middle of the flood plain of the Colorado River and therefore a poor investment. The Colorado River flows south from its headwaters at the border of Texas and New Mexico through Central Texas and on through Austin. Because of numerous floods in settlements throughout the 19th and 20th centuries, the state created the Highland Lakes system of dams in the 1930s and 1940s to manage seven lakes: Lake Buchanan, Inks Lake, Lake LBJ, Lake Marble Falls, Lake Travis, Lake Austin, and Lady Bird Lake (Town Lake), which flows alongside modern-day Zilker Park.

James Howard looked farther into Hays County and found land in Driftwood near his friend John Garrison, along Onion Creek, for $2 an acre. He bought the land in 1881 and moved his young family to their new home.

❧ DRIFTWOOD HISTORY ❧

THE RECORDED HISTORY of Driftwood, once known as Liberty Hill, and its surrounds dates back to 1826, when five Mexican land grants were formed and obtained through Ben Milam, who gained permission to establish a colony of 300 families between the Guadalupe and Colorado rivers. The area included all of Hays and Blanco counties and parts of Comal, Caldwell, Bastrop, and Travis counties. A handful of land titles were granted to people in the Driftwood area between 1826 and 1832, including the Freelove Woody land grant, which includes the present post office, the Community Center Building, a church, a cemetery, and a number of homes, farms, and ranches.

Freelove Woody was a widow with a family who received the grant as a colonist under Milam. The land was still being heavily invaded by Comanche and was hardly a place for a widow with children to make her home. Though there is no evidence that Woody ever lived on the land she was granted, she did agree to offer half of her land to William Cannon, who in exchange paid to have the property officially surveyed.

William Barrett Travis also received a land grant, in 1835, a property that included a particularly beautiful portion of Onion Creek. Before his heroic death at the Battle of the Alamo, in 1836, Travis sent back a letter to his friend in East Texas who was watching over his young son. He wrote, "Take care of my boy. If the country should be saved I may make him a splendid fortune. But if the country should be lost, and I should perish, he will have nothing but the proud recollection that he is the son of a man who died for his country."

The Comanche Indians were known to still raid the Driftwood area when settlers were making their move there in the late 1850s.

Though the whole of Travis's fortune at the time of his death is unclear, the Driftwood property he owned was inherited by his son, Charles Edward, and his daughter, Susan Isabelle. Charles later became an attorney and state representative. He found value in the great cypress trees along his Onion Creek property. As Austin was in an enormous boom at the time and cypress shingles were in high demand, he eventually sold both his and his sister's interests in the properties for a substantial profit.

Driftwood was later settled as early as the 1850s and grew in the 1880s as a supply center for neighboring ranches and farms. It eventually received its name from the logjams of driftwood that piled up in the narrows of Onion Creek from early-spring floodwaters upstream. The floodwaters delivered fertile Hill Country soil over the rocky land, along with abundant driftwood for folks to salvage. Locals drove their wagons to the large deposits of wood along the creek banks and stocked up on firewood for their farms.

The rolling hills, sweeping vistas, bubbling springs, and fertile soils deposited by the meandering Onion Creek, as well as proximity to the new rail terminals at Kyle and Buda, made Driftwood an ideal spot for ranchers and farmers. By 1890, Driftwood had its own post office but remained at a small population well into the 1990s, when the U.S. Census reported a total of 21 residents.

But back in the 1800s, Texas was a new frontier. I can't imagine the relief my great grandparents felt at finally finding their home after traveling more than 700 miles, from Mississippi to Central Texas. Yet, at the same time, how daunting was their new world. My great grandmother was only 20. I don't imagine the couple looked at each other when they picked their new homestead and said, "Honey, we're home."

Despite the dwindling Comanche population still threatening the area, the Howards managed to live safely off the land as farmers for many years. They loved their new home, and Bettie kept her promise to Howard, bearing seven more children: Minnie Myrtle (1881), Dora (1884), Grover (1886), Carl (1888), Roxie Elna (1891), Nana Irene (1893), and Charles Arthur (1896). From the 10 children came 18 grandchildren. Roxie Elna was the mother of two of them, Nana and Thurman Roberts, my father.

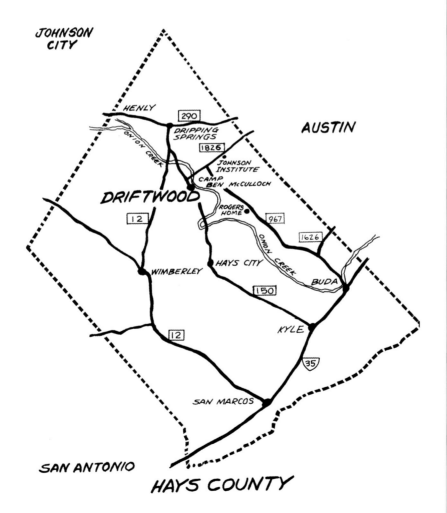

When Driftwood was originally settled in the 1850s, it was called Liberty Hill. By the 1880s it had seen a wave of new settlers from the southeastern part of the United States and became a crossroads supply center. (Map courtesy Driftwood Heritage book)

The Jim Howard
family (left to right):
Charlie, Nana,
Roxie, Carl, Dora,
Minnie, Iverson,
Lum (Columbus)
and Mrs. Howard.

⤙ ROXIE ELNA ⤚

MY GRANDMOTHER, Roxie Elna Howard, was born in 1891 and grew up with her siblings learning to work and live off the land as cotton and grain farmers. She came to know the native plants and trees; indigenous animals, from white tail deer to cotton-mouthed water moccasins; the bounty that flourished in grasses, fish, and soils from the seasonal flows of Onion Creek. As a young adult, she fell in love with a man named Bill Roberts from Gatlin. Her family did not approve of the match. Roxie was only 16 and they felt she was too young. But even at an early age, Roxie was a strong-willed woman. She dug in her heels and decided to elope with Roberts. The decision turned painful for Roxie, as her family exiled her from home, which forced her and Bill to live in Kyle. Having lived her entire life within a radius of a couple of miles, Roxie was devastated to leave her home in Driftwood. Two years later, her parents wrote her and said she had suffered long enough away from her family and her home and she was welcome to come back with Bill.

Roxie was born and raised in Driftwood and became a pillar of the social community.

Within 90 days, Roxie and Bill bought 88 acres in Driftwood, including the property where the Salt Lick is today. It was a place on a high hill overlooking the whole countryside near Camp Ben McCulloch, about a mile and a half from where she was born. They loaded up their wagons and moved from Kyle, which was no easy task, but her love for Driftwood kept her determined. They lived in a one-bedroom house with a lean-to kitchen that was already on the property. They expanded the little house over the years to accommodate their two children, Nana and Thurman.

They managed a cotton farm and a turkey farm, selling turkey eggs to a nearby turkey ranch. Roxie was a member of the Driftwood Methodist Church at an early age and volunteered for many years. She also devoted much of her time to the Order of the Eastern Star, a fraternal organization of men and women of the Freemason Society, and to raising flowers and vegetables in her garden. My grandfather, Bill, was one of the first postmasters in Driftwood and was the custodian of Camp Ben McCulloch for 50 years. The camp is one of the largest United Confederate Veterans Camps in the South, named for General Ben McCulloch, who fought for the Confederate forces during the Civil War.

My father and Aunt Nana grew up working the farm. Nana died during the Depression from blood poisoning. She was only 17. My father had left home some years before that. He wasn't able to afford more than two years of college before he quit. He left with 28 cents in his pocket and moved to Kansas City with nothing to his name, not even a job, but he eventually found work at a book publishing company. He did very well in his profession, running the press and performing a number of other jobs. But after Nana died, Roxie couldn't take it. She asked Thurman to return home, and without a second thought he left his life in Kansas City. He knew his place was with his family. To help ease her pain, he even gave Roxie a baby goat to raise, and though that didn't compare to the relief of having her son home, the baby goat was a welcome distraction for her.

Roxie passed on her love of the family's land to Thurman and taught him not only how to garden and farm and about the native plants and animals in the area but also to take pride in the land they owned. From the time he was a child through the years of my own adolescence, my family was brought together through the communal vehicle of food. Whether it was for Roxie's Sunday dinners, afternoons on the breezy banks of Onion Creek for a catfish fry, summer barbecues at the Camp Ben McCulloch "Reunions," or an early morning fire pit setup for a whole day of hog butchering and smoking, the heart of my family developed around the food and natural resources from our land.

Reluctantly, my father left home briefly for duty in World War II. The Army had been pressuring him to join, but he didn't want to be in that branch of the military. He enlisted in the Navy instead, thinking he would get off without hazardous duty. He was wrong. He was assigned to the Construction Battalion (Seabees). The Seabees were some of the first to land on the beaches during attacks of the Pacific War Theater. Their job was to move all the barricades and then to build the runways, which left them open to tremendous amounts of sniper fire. He was at battles at Saipan, Iwo Jima, and Okinawa. Afterward, he was assigned to finish his enlistment at Kaui, Hawaii, building golf courses for admirals. During his time he had earned the rank of chief petty officer, which afforded him a Jeep. He told me that I should count myself lucky he had a Jeep in the Navy. I couldn't for the life of me think why that would affect me. I later learned that his Jeep allowed him to move about the island. He frequented the Nawiliwili Harbor near Lihue, and one day he met my mother on the front porch of the general store.

She was a Hawaiian woman of Japanese descent. Her name was Hisako Tsuchiyama. Her parents had moved to Hawaii to work the pineapple fields. She and her sister, Tamie, were born in Hawaii and later graduated magna cum laude and suma cum laude, respectively, from UCLA. They returned home during the war. Tamie went on to work as an interpreter for General MacArthur's occupational staff in Japan. Hisako married my father and moved to Texas. Though she often would speak Japanese with her parents, she didn't use it much, especially once she moved to Texas.

❧ THURMAN'S WAY ❧

AT FIRST, my father started his own company as a bridge subcontractor for larger road companies. That kept the couple on the road most of the time and prevented Thurman from settling back in Driftwood immediately. During his bridge work, my brother, Thurman Lee "Butch" Roberts, Jr., was born in Greenville. I was born in Kaufman in East Texas and lived there for a few years. But in 1956, the family purchased a 580-acre working ranch on the other side of Onion Creek from the Salt Lick in Driftwood. Thurman still had to travel regularly for bridge construction, but in Driftwood we were able to be with family. Oftentimes my mother would join my father on his jobs, and my brother and I would stay with Roxie and Bill at their farmhouse. Many of my best childhood memories are from that house.

While Thurman was making good money at bridge building, his work required him to leave on Sundays, work all week on a construction site, and return on Fridays. He loved the area where he grew up and eventually realized that he simply wanted to be here, not there. One day he and Hisako took out a yellow legal pad and wrote down

Thurman Lee Roberts, Sr., Hisako Roberts, and Nickalus

54 things the family could do to stay in Driftwood. The idea for the Salt Lick was 14th on the list. Our family continued to work the ranch, farming it with grain and vegetables and raising cows and sheep. We were truck farmers for a while, growing and selling produce to area groceries in Austin, including Kash-Karry and Hyden's. We also made candies, grafted pecan trees, sold spices, and had a pecan-shelling business.

❧ THE SALT LICK BEGINS ❧

In 1967, about 100 years after the first members of the family arrived in Driftwood, Thurman took a leap into the restaurant business by opening a barbecue stand. He had already won local fame for his cooking for family events and at a barbecue stand he hosted at the Camp Ben McCulloch Reunions each year. One day he called me and our ranch hand, Guadalupe Ranchel "Lupe" Alvarado, to his favorite spot on the original homestead. He looked around a bit at the trees and location of the hill at the north side of the property and marked a spot with his boot heel in the ground. He then grabbed his barbecue fork from his truck, dug his boot heel into his mark in the dirt, and extended his arm so the tip of the barbecue fork would reach the ground. Turning slowly, he drew a circle around himself, nodded his head, and said to us, "Go grab some shovels, gravel, and cement. I want you to dig a 6-inch-wide, 6-inch-deep trench and fill it with concrete." We had no idea why, but Lupe and I did what he said.

When we finished that, he had us use rocks from the ranch to build a rock wall over this concrete footing. Only when he brought down his handmade metal grate did we realize he had directed us to build an old-fashioned smoke pit. After the pit was built, we cleared all the cedar trees from the area and took down the fence along the road so that cars could drive up to it from Ranch Road 1826.

That open pit still stands today in its original location and serves as the heartbeat for the Salt Lick restaurant. At first, it was just the pit. My father would bring meat down on Thursday nights, along with a cot and a sleeping bag. He would tend to the pit as he smoked meat all night and sleep under the stars. He would then sell barbecue all weekend until there was nothing left. He called the place the Salt Lick after a bed of big rocks in the field out where the parking lot is today. It was where we used to place nutrient minerals for the animals to browse.

My mother made side dishes up at the house and brought them down to sell too. There was no electricity, no running water, no rest rooms, and no place to sit. But people didn't seem to mind. They would drive up, order some barbecue, and perch on their car hoods or tailgates to enjoy their meal. Eventually a regular customer convinced Thurman to add a picnic table out front, and as business grew, we laid a concrete floor and built rock walls around three sides of the pit, with a wooden wall on the far end to allow us to extend the building as business grew. After 18 months in business, Thurman finally added electricity and people were able to eat with lights rather than candles and lanterns, but it would be three years before he added running water and another two years before he added rest rooms. Despite repeated encouragement to install a telephone, Thurman never acquiesced, nor did he ever advertise or seek publicity for the restaurant.

When Thurman decided to leave the bridge building industry, he and Hisako drew up a list of 54 things that they could to for a living. Creating the Salt Lick was number 14.

The original Salt Lick after a few years in business (1970s).

In his mind, the best way to build his business was through word of mouth. In the early seventies, there was no MoPac Expressway. And still, people were arriving from Austin in droves. And they did it all by word of mouth. Thurman's philosophy was, "If the food is good, people will talk about it and other people will come out. If it's no good, they won't come."

Time passed and the Salt Lick grew. And grew. What started out as a weekend barbecue shack with standing room only is now a daily lunch and dinner operation seating more than 700 and serving more than 3,000 on a Saturday or Sunday. Throughout that time our family journey has had its ups and downs. After 78 years living her life within a three-mile radius in Driftwood, Roxie passed away, as did my grandfather and my brother, Butch. I met my wife, Susan, soon after graduating college, and we welcomed my daughter, Katharine Maile Roberts, on May 25, 1984. My father had passed away in 1981, and for a number of years my mother ran the restaurant while I came in on the weekends from working in Austin to help her out. In 1987 I officially took over the restaurant.

We started to notice that people were driving in from out of town on days that we weren't open. It wasn't until the mid-nineties that we slowly began adding to our days of operation. Today we're open seven days a week, rain or shine (except on Christmas day and Thanksgiving day). For years, as the Salt Lick grew, we continued to maintain and work the 500 acres surrounding it. In 2006 I designated the remainder of that scenic expanse of land to a new development project that will enrich the property and continue the vision my family had for Driftwood.

Before Thurman's death, nearly three decades ago, he had begun building a new home, just up the hill from the Salt Lick. He built the foundation, the columns, and the framing all on his own but passed away before he could see the finished product.

Some of the Salt Lick's first employees included Scott Roberts (third from the left) and his brother, "Butch" Roberts (third from the right).

Years later, I was able to pick up where he left off and finish his house, which now overlooks the restaurant, 50 acres of vineyards, a burgeoning home community, and miles and miles of Texas hills and valleys. The house, appropriately named Thurman's Mansion, is now our offices and the venue where we host events and weddings.

Today, as I gaze out over the landscape from the second-story balcony, I'm reminded of how my family has cared for this land for more than 100 years. They wanted their property and their home to be enjoyable and well kept so that people could see how proud of it they were. And that sentiment transcends just my family to many of the other families around here. There was always a desire to do the best with what they had.

It's a way of life that extends back to the kitchen. You would be sautéing something, and if it burned a little, you started over. Without that type of care, you will never make a good dish. It doesn't matter what recipe you have or what ingredients you have, because without that overwhelming desire to do the best you can with what you've got, you don't have anything. That's why my grandmother was such a good cook and why you wanted to be her guest at her Sunday dinners. That's why my father and mother built a restaurant that still exemplifies that and has grown over the years. It is instilled in me through my family. And that's why the story behind the Salt Lick is really a story about family. It began with my great grandparents, my grandparents, and my parents, and it continues through me and my daughter, Maile. She married in the Salt Lick vineyards on October 22, 2011, to begin her family story on this land.

What's the secret to a good dish? Ultimately, the answer is you. If you respect the land around you, respect all the little ingredients that go into the dish to make it right— and the hard work and effort it took to make those ingredients—and respect the very heritage that made you what you are today, then you hold the key to great food.

ROXIE'S HOUSE

★ ★ ★

ROXIE WAS MY GRANDMOTHER. She and my grandfather, Bill, lived across the road from us, but I spent much of my childhood at her house. My parents traveled a lot for my dad's bridge construction jobs when I was little, and Roxie and my grandfather would take care of my brother, Butch, and me. Many of my fondest childhood memories are from her house, which still stands today. She taught me how to garden, how to make sausage, how to prepare fresh vegetables, and how to catch fireflies in mason jars in the summertime. She also taught me how not to be lazy. For her and my grandfather, it was a sin to be in bed. They got up before the sun rose and didn't quit working their ranch until after sunset, even on holidays. Where my great grandparents, James and Bettie Howard, laid the foundation for our family history, Roxie and Bill worked hard to build the framework—brick by brick and meal by meal.

When I was little, Roxie had me watch her make dinner in her kitchen. When it was ready, she would tell me to go call my grandfather while he was working outside. I'd run to the front door and call him, but all I could say at the time was "Oooo." And when I tried to say her name, all that came out was "Ga ga." As happens with most little kids, "Grand-father" and "Grandmother" were just too difficult to say. So for the first part of my life, I knew them as Ooo and Ga Ga, but as I got older, Ga Ga became Roxie to me.

Roxie was a lovely woman. She had an antique vanity in her room, and I used to watch her stroke her long gray and auburn–streaked hair 100 times with her brush as she got ready for bed. She was a good seamstress and made her own dresses. They always looked matronly, but she wasn't really into fashion. She did like to get dressed up and have friends and family over to entertain. She loved to cook big meals, especially on Sundays, when we would all come over and eat at her big oak table. The adults would sit for hours and talk in the living room or on the front porch while we kids played around outside.

All of my cousins were much older, so my brother and I were really the only young kids around. Because we stayed with Roxie so much, I think she looked at us as her own. She lost her daughter, Nana, at 17, and I don't think she ever got over it. I think she invested in us as though we were her own sons, and I think it helped fill that void for her.

Roxie would always cook a nice breakfast for us and make cookies, hot chocolate, or popcorn after dinner when we were staying there. When we were little, we slept with her in her big bed in the wintertime when it was cold. She would rub our arms and legs to warm us up before bed. When we got up in the morning, there was always a fire going in the fireplace. She asked my grandfather to get up first in the mornings, saying, "Bill, get up and get the fire started so the kids won't be cold."

Roxie was committed to her family, but she also had a mind of her own. She was kind and hardworking, and I don't remember her ever getting upset, except for one time when I hid from her. My grandparents had a turkey farm with more than 500 turkeys in a back pasture. They each had their own little coop to lay their eggs. There was a big fence to keep them all in, with rock columns and a gate. It was loud. You could hear them gobbling all throughout the day, but as a little one, I loved watching them run around, with their heads bobbing up and down.

One day, I went out to help pick eggs. There was a hen out of the coop, and I crawled into the back of the coop. When the hen came back, she wouldn't let me out and kept pecking at me. I hid as far back in the coop as I could to get away from it, but it ripped my clothes and gave me scrapes and bruises. Everyone, my parents, my grandparents, were looking for me. I was gone for hours. It was a long time before they found me, crying and terrified at the back of that coop. I remember hearing Roxie yelling and crying for me when they were looking for me. I'd never heard her cry before. She was really upset. After they found me, she cleaned me up and got me in fresh clothes. She made my favorite treat—popcorn made in a square cast-iron pot in the fireplace—and doted on me all evening.

But then I made the mistake of hiding again a few days later in hopes of getting the same attention from her. It backfired. Instead of a bath and a nice meal, I got a whipping. Looking back, I think both reactions from her were evidence of how much she cared about me.

PREVIOUS SPREAD: Bill and Roxie Roberts' turn-of-the-century home still stands today. This is where Roxie's famed Sunday dinners were held, where a field of turkeys were farmed just behind, and where Scott Roberts spent many of his fondest childhood days.

On the weekends, Roxie would get dressed up and go to the Eastern Star. Sometimes she'd bring me with her to get a little exposure to "society." She always made a special chicken salad sandwich with grapes and pecans. It was so delicious. She was pretty social in the Driftwood area. She would go to community events, and she went to church every Sunday.

My grandfather was the custodian of Camp Ben McCulloch for 50 years, and we were always involved with its annual summer Reunion. It was a big deal for families of Confederate veterans. Everyone would stake out their special spot to camp on the property, and we all spent a few weeks mingling with different people, cooking out, and camping under the stars.

I don't remember much about my grandfather, Bill. He kept to himself. He read the paper and *Reader's Digest*. He would sit on the porch a lot and listen to baseball games on the radio. He loved baseball. In fact, I think that was the only thing

Stone and concrete picnic tables along the historic grounds of Camp Ben McCulloch.

that ever really got him excited. There used to be a gigantic grandstand in Austin, and he would always go to those games. There aren't many places he ever went: to the turkey ranch to deliver turkey eggs, to the feed store in Austin where Guero's restaurant is now, to take Roxie to get groceries, and to the baseball games at that grandstand. He loved going to those games. Other than that, he didn't go anywhere.

It seemed to me that all he ever wanted to do was read his paper, have a car, and go to baseball games. He hardly ever talked. I remember when he did talk, I would look at him in surprise. I think maybe he just didn't really relate to kids, but I guess he didn't really have to. Most of my time was spent with Roxie.

The house they lived in was built around 1900. It was small at first, with only a couple of rooms and a porch, but they eventually extended it to have a separate kitchen from the living room. They also added a wide screen porch at the front door. Most of our leisure time was spent on that porch. It had a swing and two rocking chairs for my grandparents, and it always caught breezes from the pastures that swept across the concrete floor. I used to lie on that concrete floor during the hot summers and try to get cool as the breezes blew through.

In the kitchen Roxie had a little refrigerator and a small table to work on. She always insisted on using rainwater for cooking and washing her hair, even after we got a well, in 1948. She never liked the well water; she said it tasted hard. If we ran out of rainwater, she'd make us take the truck to Onion Creek for water. They also had a small icebox outside to keep things cool.

Out back, along the side of the house, Roxie had a garden. She was forever tending the garden, which brimmed with vegetables by the season. I remember helping her with cucumbers, onions, corn, squash, and black-eyed peas. I remember the first time I had black-eyed peas from a can and wondered why in the world people ate them that way. Having had Roxie's fresh black-eyed peas, I was certain there was no better way. In the summertime, she had little cherry tomatoes that would get warm in the sun. When you put them in your mouth, they burst with warm, sweet juice. It was one of the best treats of the summer.

Roxie had a big heart. She was one of the few people who would say "thank you" when you helped her in the kitchen or with her garden. The time I spent with Roxie was more than just learning how to prune a garden or how to make her famous fried chicken. It wasn't until later in life that I realized what she was really teaching me— how to care for your family and the place where you lived. The time she invested in her home and the land around her was equal to the time she invested in me. It showed me the importance in taking pride in the place you come from.

A few years ago, I was driving through the parking lot of the Salt Lick, and I stopped my truck to get out and pick up cigarette butts people had left behind. Someone walked by me and said, "You own this place, don't you?" And I said, "Yeah, how did you know?" And he said, "Because it's obvious that you care about it."

That person recognized the values Roxie had instilled in me when I was just a little boy. They are values that I treasure to this day and hope I have passed on to my family as well.

The porch at Roxie's house is where my grandfather would sit and read his newspapers and Reader's Digest *magazines. He didn't talk much, but with all the reading he did, I'm sure he had a lot of knowledge stored up that I never got to hear.*

This is the living room where Roxie would host her Sunday dinners. She would add leaves to this table to expand seating to include the whole family and a few friends as well.

❧ SUNDAY DINNERS ❧

AN INVITATION TO Roxie's house for Sunday dinner was a special treat. She had a round oak table in the main room of her house that sat about eight people. Sunday dinner at Roxie's was special, mainly because the food was so good but also because it was a rare occasion when I was little to have my whole family together, since my dad often traveled for business. She would begin preparing the meal in the hours before Sunday church and finish the main cooking while we played out in the front yard and the adults visited on the front porch. The menu usually included an endless platter of crisp fried chicken (though sometimes she made a roast), accompanied by fresh vegetables from her garden, mashed potatoes, and warm biscuits.

FRIED CHICKEN

AS MUCH AS I loved eating her food, I remember not being a fan of watching the preparation. As a kid, it seemed tedious to me to have to stem the green beans, shuck the corn, mash the potatoes. But she did it all. Even the chicken. That was my least favorite. She would take a chicken from the backyard and chop its head off. And, yes, they do still run around after they've lost their head. It didn't really scare me to see it flopping around with blood all over the place. What scared me was having to clean it. She would dip the chicken in scalding water and then de-feather it. I don't believe I can remember a worse smell than wet chicken feathers. It was awful. I remember wondering why in the world people would want to stuff their pillows with those foul-smelling things and then sleep on them. But by the time we were seated around the table, staring at the large plate of golden fried chicken, with aromatic steam wafting throughout the room, I had forgotten all that it took to get there.

Roxie prepared her fried chicken in a very simple manner, but it was so good! A cast-iron skillet, lard, bacon grease, salt, pepper, and flour was all she needed to turn her farm-raised chicken into some of the best Sunday eating in the county. You could taste all of the work she put into it. She fussed over the skillet, she fussed over getting the fire just right for the stove. I have vivid memories of her slaving over that stove.

Her chickens were not the chickens of today; they were smaller and tougher. Sometimes if the chicken she chose was older, she would simmer it in a pot until it was tender and then fry it. The chickens had almost no breasts but large thighs and legs from scratching in the grass for their worms, insects, and corn. Today's chicken breasts are so large you might need to cut them in half so that they get done before the crust burns.

If the taste of fried chicken is what you are after, try this simple recipe. The flour gives the skin and outside a little crunch, the pepper and salt lightly season, and the oils and the frying process tenderize and bring out the flavor of the chicken so that when you finish, you really taste the chicken.

But you can also play with this recipe. So many flavors can be added with brines and marinades, basil, thyme, orange honey, wildflower honey, cayenne, and serrano, to name a few. In the crust you can imbed the flavor of garlic, onion, black pepper, cayenne, or chipotle. The crust can be made thicker by dipping the chicken in milk or buttermilk and even thicker by double dipping and dredging.

This is Roxie's old-fashioned recipe.

1 whole chicken, rinsed and divided
Salt and white pepper, enough to season the chicken well
2 cups flour
1 to 1½ cups lard, plus 2 tablespoons bacon grease for flavoring,
    enough to fill ½ to ¾ of a large cast-iron skillet

Wash chicken, pat dry, and season with salt and white pepper. Dredge in flour and shake off excess. *NOTE: If you find flour alone too bland, add a little of the seasoning mix on page 88 to the flour.* Heat bacon grease and sweet lard in cast-iron skillet to about 350 degrees. Lay legs and thighs skin down and fry for 6 minutes, turn, and add breasts and wings, skin down. Fry for an additional 6 minutes. Turn, and fry for an additional 3 minutes. Remove to wire rack or plate covered with paper towels. Make sure to place the chicken skin side up after it is fried. These times are relative; some may cook a bit quicker and some may take a little longer.

ROXIE'S PAN GRAVY

ROXIE MADE this gravy in the pan after she finished frying different meats. It is very versatile. In the mornings you can crumble sausage into it and serve over biscuits. At lunch and dinner it is great over chicken-fried steak or venison. On Sunday, when it is made in the fried chicken pan, it is good with hot buttery mashed potatoes.

PAN GRAVY TIP: When you make cream gravy, the best way to keep from forming clumps is to use very cold water or milk and to stir vigorously. You may have to try it a few times to get it just right. As they say, practice makes perfect.

For 1 cup:
2 tablespoons fat (meat drippings)
1½ tablespoons Gold Medal Wondra flour
1 cup cold water or milk
Salt and pepper to taste

Remove frying pan from heat and pour off fat (do not clean pan); measure amount needed and add back to pan. Add flour, and stir into fat. Pour in cold liquid. Stir to blend thoroughly. Return to heat, and while stirring constantly bring to a boil. Boil for 1 minute. Season to taste and serve.

MASHED POTATOES

WITH GA GA, butter was king. The secret to her mashed potatoes is to boil the potatoes in their jackets. That seals in moisture and makes the potatoes creamy when you mash them. It was a simple recipe: potatoes, salt, pepper, butter, butter, and butter. You can always add things like garlic, horseradish, or bleu cheese, but why would you, when you can have the perfect taste of potatoes and butter, butter, and butter?

½ pound butter
2 pounds russet potatoes
Salt and pepper to taste

Bring butter to room temperature and whip slightly. Boil potatoes in their skins until a fork easily slides in. Pour off all water, and cover pot. Dip one potato at a time in ice water bath, remove peel, and place in covered pot or dish. Once all potatoes are peeled, begin to mash and add whipped butter until all potatoes are mashed and all butter is incorporated. Season with salt and fresh ground black pepper to taste.

ROXIE'S QUICK BISCUITS

FOR ROXIE'S BISCUITS, the most important element had nothing to do with the ingredients, but with preheating the oven. In some of her original recipe notes, she always made the point to get the oven heated just right. It finally dawned on me that she wasn't using the same type of oven we preheat today. She had a wood-fired oven. She would have to start a fire and wait for the temperature to get just right. It took almost an hour and a half to preheat her oven, which means it was crucial to get the oven just right before she even mixed the dough for the biscuits.

This is how Roxie said to do it. She didn't really measure. She just made a hole in some sifted flour, cut in the butter, added the wet ingredients, pushed in the flour, mixed until it was the consistency she wanted, rolled, and baked.

¼ cup softened butter
4 cups sifted flour (White Lily is best)
2 teaspoons baking powder
1 teaspoon salt
2 tablespoons sugar
1 teaspoon baking soda
1 pint buttermilk

Preheat oven to 400 degrees. Cut butter into flour and baking powder. Stir salt, sugar, and baking soda into buttermilk, and add it to the flour. Stir quickly. Using 2 large spoons, scoop individual-sized drop biscuits into a baking dish ½ inch apart, or roll out the dough about ½ inch thick and cut out with a biscuit cutter; bake immediately in a quick oven.

Roxie's living room was the heart of the home, but it was outside in her gardens, in the fields, and throughout the expansive boundaries of Driftwood that kept the family strong.

A NOTE ON FLOUR
There are all types of flour to use when making biscuits. Roxie and Hisako both swore by White Lily. If you can find it, it makes all the difference.

BISCUIT HOW-TO:
(See Hisako's Biscuits on page 41 for full recipe)
[1] First, measure out all ingredients and use a wide bread bowl to mix them together. Be sure to preheat the oven as well. [2] Pour flour onto mixing board or bowl.

[3] Add the soft butter to the flour. [4] Begin to incorporate the butter and create a small depression in the flour in a bowl shape. [5] Add baking soda and baking powder, and combine well. [6] Dissolve yeast in warm water; add to buttermilk, and pour into flour. [7-8] Combine well, making sure all ingredients are incorporated. [9] Roll the dough into a loose ball. [10] Sprinkle flour onto a hard surface to roll the dough. [11] Place the dough on floured surface.

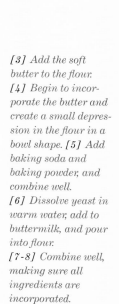

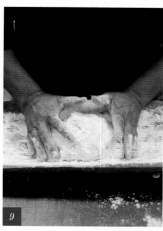

[12] Gently and slowly, roll the dough into a round shape.
[13] The dough should be rolled to 1 inch in thickness.
[14] Spot check the dough to make sure it is uniform in thickness with no breaks.
[15] Place a dry cloth over the dough and let rest for 2 hours.
[16] Use a large biscuit cutter to form individual biscuits.
[17] Gently remove the individual biscuits from the rolled dough.
[18] The biscuits should be thick and light, not dense.
[19] Place biscuits in a cast-iron skillet or on a baking sheet.
[20] Reroll remaining dough to cut remaining biscuits.
[21] Arrange biscuits closely together.

HISAKO'S BISCUITS

WHILE ROXIE MADE large flat biscuits, Hisako made light fluffy ones. Having spent so much time between their two houses, I find it difficult to say which were my favorite, but these were pretty hard to beat, smeared with butter and my mother's homemade jams.

  5 cups unsifted flour
  ¼ cup sugar
  3 teaspoons baking powder
  1 teaspoon baking soda
  1½ teaspoon salt
  1 cup shortening
  1 package dry yeast
  2 tablespoons warm water
  2 cups buttermilk

Sift dry ingredients together, then cut in shortening. Dissolve yeast in warm water, and add to buttermilk. Then add to dry ingredients. Cover and refrigerate (will keep several weeks).

Preheat oven to 400 degrees. Roll amount to be baked to 1 inch thick on slightly floured board. Cut and place on greased sheet pan; grease biscuit tops. Let stand 1 to 2 hours to rise. Bake for 15 minutes. Makes 3 dozen.

SCOTT'S BEATEN BISCUITS

WHEN I WAS YOUNG, Roxie let me play at making biscuits. I couldn't make hers, so she gave me this recipe. I got them right once and from then on they were known as Scott's Biscuits.

  2 quarts sifted flour
  1 teaspoon salt
  1 tablespoon lard (butter is fine if you prefer not to use lard)
  1 egg mixed with ½ pint whole milk

Preheat oven to 400 degrees. Mix together all ingredients. Beat until dough blisters and cracks. Pull off 2-inch square of dough. Roll individual biscuits into ball with your hands and place on a greased baking sheet. Flatten, stick with a fork for air, and bake in a quick oven until browned.

It is not beating hard that makes the biscuit nice, but the regularity of the motion. Beating hard, as the old cooks say, kills the dough.

All three of these recipes yield very different biscuits, but they all represent a different memory. Try each one out to see which you like the most.

CREAM GRAVY

I'VE INCLUDED this recipe because it works better with breakfast biscuits. It's especially good with crumbled bits of breakfast sausage or chopped smoked brisket in it. For fried chicken, use the pan gravy instead.

4 tablespoons butter
5 tablespoons flour
2 ½ cups milk
2 teaspoons salt
2 to 3 teaspoons ground pepper

Melt butter over medium low heat in medium-sized saucepot. Whisk flour into butter for about 5 minutes, until smooth. Slowly add milk, and stir constantly until smooth. Season to taste, and stir often for about 10 minutes, until the gravy has thickened.

CREAMED CORN

½ onion, diced
1 tablespoon butter
2 pinches kosher salt
8 ears fresh corn
1 tablespoon sugar
2 tablespoons yellow cornmeal
1 cup heavy cream
Fresh ground black pepper

In a medium pan over medium high heat, sauté onion and butter until onion is translucent. Add salt.

Use sharp knife to slice tops of corn kernels off corncobs. Then go back with the dull edge of the knife to scrape the remaining pulp and corn milk into a bowl. This is where the flavor is. Add kernels and pulp mixture to pan, and cook over medium high. Sprinkle corn with sugar. Stir constantly for about 2 minutes. Sprinkle on cornmeal, using a whisk to combine well. Add heavy cream, and cook until corn has softened, 2 to 3 minutes. Season with pepper.

ROXIE'S ON-THE-FLY CUCUMBER SALAD

Roxie would make two kinds of salad with her fresh-grown cucumbers, one for dinner and the other when she was in a hurry for lunch. When she was in a hurry, she would just use fresh cucumbers and onions, lemon juice, white pepper, sugar, and vinegar. Just slice and chop cucumbers and onions, mix together with next 3 ingredients, cover with vinegar, and refrigerate for 15 minutes. Pour off vinegar, place salad in bowl, and serve. I had her add sliced tomatoes to mine, but no one else liked it that way. I couldn't ever find quantities for this recipe because Roxie always made it on the fly and it took whatever amount she was in the mood for at the moment. Pick, wash, slice, chop, mix, refrigerate, drain, and serve. That is how she made her on-the-fly salad: simple, but oh-so-tasty. This is my best guess:

  3 large cucumbers
  ½ purple onion, diced
  ½ to 1 teaspoon sugar
  ¼ to ½ teaspoon white pepper
  White vinegar to cover salad in a bowl

Slice cucumbers in ¼-inch slices. Add purple onion, sugar, and white pepper. Stir and cover with vinegar. Refrigerate about 30 minutes. Drain off vinegar, stir, and serve.

DINNER CUCUMBER SALAD

  3 large cucumbers, peeled and sliced ¼-inch thick
  Salt water, enough to soak above ingredients in a bowl
  1 small purple onion, chopped
  Vinegar, enough to soak above ingredients in a bowl
  ½ teaspoon sugar
  ¼ teaspoon white pepper
  2 teaspoons lemon juice
  ½ cup sour cream
  2 stalks fresh dill, chopped

Soak sliced cucumbers in salt water for 30 minutes, drain well, rinse quickly, and drain. Add onion. Marinate in vinegar for 30 minutes in refrigerator; drain well. Sprinkle with sugar, pepper, and lemon juice. Mix and fold in sour cream. Chill. Sprinkle dill over mixture, and serve.

SELECTING THE RIGHT VEGETABLES
Roxie's Sunday dinners were dictated by the vegetables that were showing best in her garden. Depending on the season, this could have been fresh tomatoes, cucumber, spinach, or asparagus.

❧ VEGETABLES ❧

ROXIE'S FRONT YARD was always nicely manicured. It didn't have over-embellished landscaping, but the grass was always green and lush and it was cut so that the whole front yard looked clean. You could run barefoot through the grass, and the soft cool blades would massage your feet. In the backyard, she had a large garden, where she grew all sorts of vegetables. Whatever was in season is what she used to make vegetable dishes for Sunday dinners. When I was a young boy, she always asked me to help her in the garden, picking squash, okra, or zucchini, pulling weeds, or helping her plant the next season's crop. I spent a lot of time working on that garden. Sometimes I can almost taste the perfect flavors that came out of that little plot of land.

COUNTRY SQUASH BAKE

ROXIE LOVED yellow squash fresh from her backyard garden. She cooked it many ways, fried or stewed in batter with onions or in this baked dish. I liked this dish because even with the other core ingredients, the star of the dish is the squash.

10 large yellow squash, cut into ¼-inch wheels
½ cup chopped onion
8 ounces sour cream
½ teaspoon salt
½ teaspoon basil
⅛ teaspoon cayenne pepper
1 cup cracker crumbs
½ cup shredded cheddar cheese
¼ cup unsalted butter, melted and cooled
½ teaspoon paprika

Place squash and onion in pan, and add water to cover. Bring to boil, cover, and cook 10 to 15 minutes, or until tender. Drain well and lightly mash. Combine squash mixture, sour cream, and next 3 ingredients, and mix well. Ladle into greased 2-quart casserole.

Preheat oven to 300 degrees. Combine cracker crumbs and remaining 3 ingredients; toss well. Sprinkle over squash. Bake uncovered for 30 minutes or until crust is firm and dish is thoroughly heated. Serves 6 to 8.

Summer squash was one of the great bounties that came from Roxie's garden. This dish was almost a meal unto itself.

FRIED OKRA

FRIED OKRA

6 cups oil, approximately
½ cup cornmeal
1 cup all-purpose flour
1 tablespoon garlic salt
1 teaspoon white pepper
¼ teaspoon cayenne pepper
2 pounds fresh okra, sliced ½-inch thick
½ cup buttermilk

Heat oil in a large heavy-bottomed skillet or Dutch oven to 350 degrees. (You may not need to use this much oil; do not fill the pan over half.)

In a medium bowl, combine cornmeal, flour, garlic salt, and peppers. Dip okra in buttermilk, then dredge in cornmeal-flour mixture to coat well. Carefully add okra to hot oil, and cook until golden brown. (It may be necessary to fry in batches.) Remove from oil, drain on paper towels, and serve immediately.

ROXIE'S GREENS

WHEN I WAS younger, greens—whether collard, turnip, or mustard—were always bitter to me. As I got older, they tasted better and better, especially when cooked with pieces of ham hock meat. This preparation works on all greens. I have also included another greens recipe that is faster and lighter and incorporates our smoked turkey. Try them both, and see which one you like the best. Not for sentimental reasons but for taste reasons, I like Roxie's the best.

1 large ham hock, one that will yield about a cup of lean meat
1 large bunch greens
1 tablespoon bacon fat
Salt and pepper

Wash greens thoroughly. They can be very dirty and gritty. Remove the stems that run down the center by holding the leaf in your left hand and stripping the leaf down with your right hand. Repeat on the other side. The tender young leaves do not need to be stripped. Stack 6 to 8 leaves, roll up, and slice into ½- to 1-inch-thick slices.

In a large pot, place ham hock, cover with water, and bring to a boil. Add greens and cook until tender. Turnip and mustard will cook faster than collards.

Remove greens and ham hock. Remove lean meat from the ham hock and shred into bite-size pieces. In a cast-iron skillet, add bacon fat and cook ham hock meat over medium heat until crusty. Add greens and stir. Season, remove to platter, and serve.

SMOKED TURKEY GREENS

2 tablespoons unsalted butter

1 shallot, minced

1 bunch of greens, hard stems removed and cut into ½- to 1-inch strips

¼ cup chicken stock

½ cup diced smoked turkey

1 teaspoon unsalted butter

2 tablespoons freshly squeezed lemon juice (for collard greens;
    use 1 tablespoon for mustard and turnip greens)

⅛ teaspoon red chile flakes

¼ teaspoon kosher salt or sea salt

1 teaspoon toasted sesame seeds

Melt 2 tablespoons butter in large cast-iron skillet over medium heat. Add shallots and cook until tender, about 1 minute. Add greens, stirring occasionally, and cook about 3 minutes or until greens are wilted. Add chicken stock and smoked turkey, and cook 3 more minutes. Add 1 teaspoon butter, lemon juice, chile flakes, and salt. Toss well, plate, sprinkle with sesame seeds, and serve.

Some days, the Texas summers were so hot, the only refuge was on Roxie's front porch, where there always seemed to be a breeze and the concrete floor was always cool.

COLLARD AND TURNIP GREENS

The view of Roxie's backyard. There was a time when these fields were filled with little turkey houses when the family ran a turkey farm.

ROUND-CUT FRENCH FRIES

THESE WERE a special treat at Sunday dinners. Instead of making long-cut fries, Roxie cut the potatoes into thick rounds and fried them up. They were like gigantic potato chips. I don't have Roxie's recipe, but a few years ago I had a side of Brabant potatoes at Austin's Eddie V's restaurant, downtown. The first time I had them, I immediately thought of Roxie. This is the Eddie V's recipe. Roxie would have served just the crisp potatoes without the sautéed onions.

> Peanut oil for frying, enough to cover 1 to 2 inches in a frying pan
> 2 cups potatoes, boiled, peeled, sliced to ¼-inch thickness
> ½ cup sliced onion
> 2 ounces butter
> Salt and pepper to taste
> Chopped parsley for garnish

In a deep frying skillet, bring peanut oil to 350 degrees. Fry potatoes until crisp and golden brown. Set aside on a plate lined with a paper towel.

In a separate skillet, sauté onions in butter until translucent, add potatoes, and season. Toss well, garnish with parsley, and serve hot.

BREAD

ROXIE MADE the best homemade bread. At least, it seemed like the best bread in the world after coming home from working the ranch all morning. Good bread was served with just about everything, but it wasn't easy to make. You were somebody if you could make good bread, and Roxie made the best. I remember the earthenware bowl she let the dough rest in after she kneaded it and the damp cloth she used to cover the bowl to let the dough rise. In the winter she would find a warm spot near the wood-burning stove to let it sit, and in the summer she would find a cool spot in the kitchen. I was always curious about what happened under that cloth while she waited hours to work with the dough again. I loved watching her punch the dough down after it had been sitting for a while. The great *whoosh* of air that escaped the air pockets fascinated me.

My favorite part was the smell that filled the kitchen when she took the bread from the oven. It would raise a pang of hunger in you that could almost knock you over. I wanted so badly to grab the bread while it was still hissing and popping from the steam inside. We were always pestering her to let us have a piece right away. One time she said to me, "Hush, hush, little one. Let it rest. When it quits talkin', it's ready." Once the bread was finished, she cut me a big warm slice and spread butter all over it, letting it melt into the air pockets. I would happily run out to the front yard and devour it while the cool grass cushioned my bare feet.

½ cup warm water (105–115 degrees F)
1 tablespoon active dry yeast
4 tablespoons sugar
2 cups warm water
1 tablespoon salt
5½–6 cups bread flour or all-purpose flour
½ cup unsalted butter, softened

Pour ½ cup water into a mixing bowl and add yeast and sugar. Let sit for 5 minutes until creamy. Add to the bowl the rest of the water, salt, and 3½ cups of the flour, and knead (with dough hook if using a mixer) on medium speed until blended, then add 2 cups of the flour and fully incorporate. Continue kneading, then add butter 1 tablespoon at a time (dough may come apart, but mixing will pull it back together). If dough is still too sticky, add ¼ cup of flour at a time (you should need no more than 6 cups total) and knead (by hand or with dough hook), about 10 minutes, until dough is smooth and elastic and comes away from the sides.

Shape dough into a ball, and place in large buttered or oiled bowl. Turn dough so it is completely coated in butter and cover in plastic for 45 minutes to 1 hour, until it has doubled in size, at room temperature. Deflate dough (punch down), turn onto lightly floured surface, and cut in half. Roll out into two 9 x 12–inch rectangles. Butter two loaf pans. With the narrow end of dough facing you, fold the dough into thirds lengthwise, creating a roll. Pinch the seam closed, and pinch the ends enough so it will fit in the loaf pan. Drop in loaf pan, seam side down, and repeat. Cover the loaves with buttered plastic wrap and allow them to rise again in a warm place (80 degrees F) for 45 minutes, until they double in size. Preheat oven to 375 degrees F, and place rack in center of oven. Bake 35 to 45 minutes, until loaves are honey brown. Immediately turn out of pans onto a rack to cool. Once almost completely cool, they can be cut. Store slices in a brown paper bag for a day or two. Once cut, turn the loaf cut side down onto a cutting board and cover with a kitchen towel.

Let the Bread Quit Talkin'

When Roxie made homemade bread while I was growing up, I was always eager to get a slice right when it came out of the oven. But she always told me to let it "quit talkin'" before we could have some. It wasn't until many years later, when I was reading a cookbook called *The Lahey Method for No-Knead Bread in a Pot*, that I learned that the talkin' was part of the last phase of bread cooking once it is pulled from the oven. According to Lahey, "the exterior of the loaf is very dry the moment it's removed, but the interior is still wet. During cooling, the two elements of the bread start to even out somewhat, although the crust will remain brittle, and the crumb soft. The crust is shrinking and cracking. Steam escapes from the cracks, which is the racket you hear, as it forces its way through, while the crumb solidifies. At this point the bread seems alive."

That is why you have to wait for bread to quit talkin'. When you pull it out of the oven, it still has a ways to go before it is finished cooking, usually just a few minutes.

BREAD HOW-TO:
[1] Measure and set out all ingredients and preheat oven.
[2] Pour ½ cup of water into a small mixing bowl.

[3] Add the dry yeast to the water.
[4] Stir in sugar and let sit for 5 minutes until creamy.
[5] In a large mixing bowl, add flour and remaining water.
[6] Add the yeast and water mixture.
[7] Add salt and begin to knead ingredients together.
[8] While kneading the dough, add butter.
[9] Combine ingredients well. You can use an electric mixer with a dough hook as well.
[10] Cover the dough with a cloth or plastic, and leave to rise until it doubles in size. [11] Grease bread pans with butter.

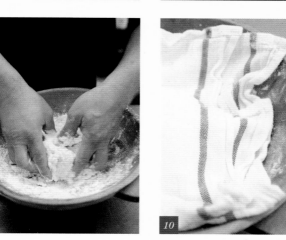

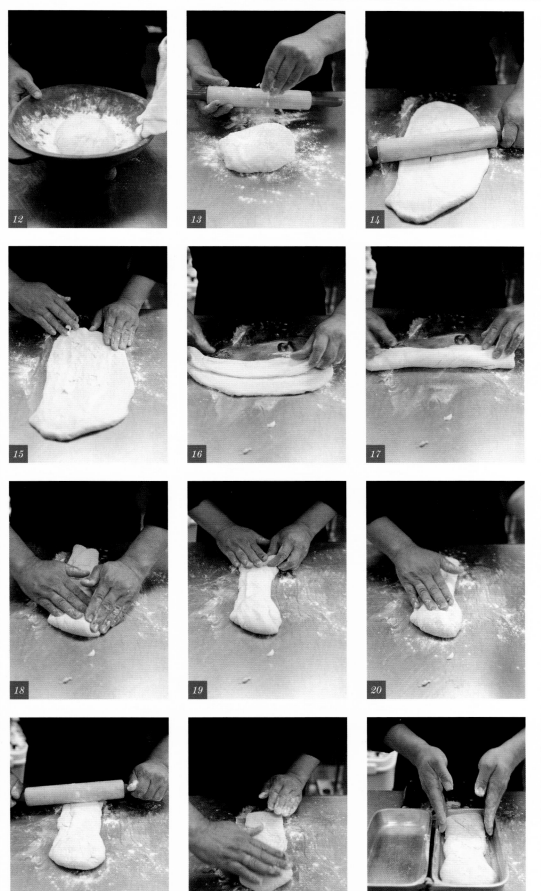

[12] Punch the dough and round into a ball shape. [13] Flour a hard surface and rolling pin. [14] Begin rolling the dough. [15] Be sure to sprinkle dough with flour to keep from sticking. [16 & 17] Fold the dough in thirds. [18 & 19] Pat the dough to seal the folded seams. [20] Flour the dough to keep from sticking.

[21] Gently roll the folded dough. [22] Carefully lift the dough from the table. [23] Place dough in a bread pan.

❧ LUNCH SANDWICHES ❧

ROXIE WOULD always have lunch for us with fresh bread that left its heavenly scent throughout the house. She usually made all sorts of sandwiches for lunch. I would eat and then lie on the concrete porch to cool off a little before going back to work. My grandfather sat in a rocking chair and read the paper. He wasn't much of a conversationalist. One of our few conversations happened while I was lying on that porch floor. I was reading a *Reader's Digest* while he read the newspaper, and I saw a story on destinations around the world. I told him—or the open newspaper that was perpetually in front of his face—that I would really like to go to Paris or Athens one day. He remained quiet for a few minutes, and I was wondering if he had even heard me. Eventually, the paper lowered and there he sat, with a funny look on his face. Then he said, "Son, why in the hell would you want to go to East Texas?"

HAM SALAD SANDWICH

Roxie's bread was so good, it almost didn't matter what you put in between two slices to make a sandwich. Smoked ham is also a good substitution for this recipe.

ROXIE MADE a wonderful ham salad with her leftover Sunday Dinner hams. As with most of her dishes, it is simple but the taste of the main ingredient, the ham, really comes out. I believe her secret ingredient, outside of the ham, was sweet pickles she made from her fresh garden cucumbers.

  2 cups chopped leftover ham
  1 cup finely diced celery
  ¼ cup finely minced sweet onion
  1 teaspoon mustard
  1 hard-boiled egg, diced
  ¼ cup chopped sweet pickle
  ¼ cup good quality mayonnaise

Mix all ingredients until well blended.

Roxie toasted thick slices of her homemade bread on a grill over the wood fire of her cook stove. She spread on the ham salad and topped it with slices of ripe red homegrown tomatoes and purple onions. You could add some crisp lettuce, but she didn't.

Other additions are:

  ¼ cup chopped toasted pecans
  ¼ teaspoon chopped pickled jalapeños
  ¼ teaspoon minced fresh dill

When Hill Country peaches are in season, I chop up ½ of a skinned peach, add ⅛ teaspoon fresh serranos, lightly cover with sugar, stir, and substitute this for the pecans and chopped pickled jalapeños. Peaches and ham: a great sandwich.

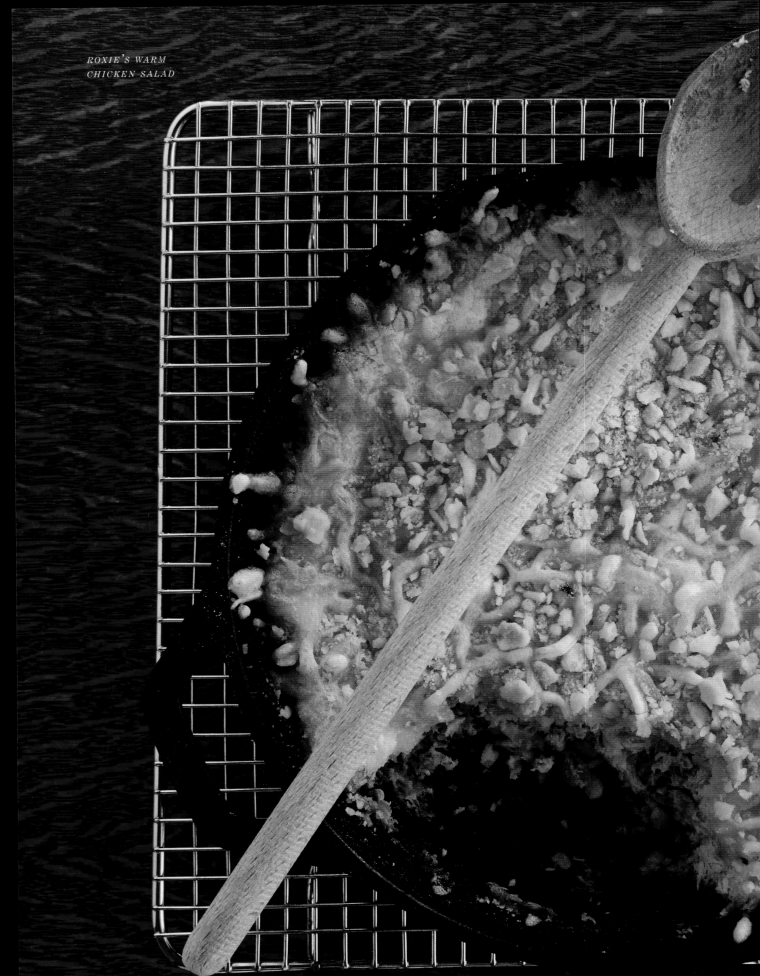

ROXIE'S WARM CHICKEN SALAD

MY GRANDMOTHER was a member of the Order of the Eastern Star, which is an organization of Freemasons that began in the mid-1800s. The group met in Dripping Springs for community events, and she would always bring something to eat for the meetings. I remember little triangle-shaped sandwiches she made from a leftover chicken salad casserole recipe. It was a warm chicken salad that was delicious just out of the oven, but it was also great served cold on her white bread. We've used her recipe many times as inspiration for chicken salad appetizers at different catering events. It's particularly good if you use smoked chicken.

3 cups chopped cooked chicken
2 cups chopped celery
½ cup toasted pecans
2 tablespoon lemon juice
½ cup Miracle Whip
½ cup sour cream
2 tablespoon chopped onion
½ cup grated American cheese
Sliced Swiss cheese
Pepper and salt
Buttered cracker crumbs
Macaroni, optional

Preheat oven to 350 degrees. Combine chicken, celery, pecans, and lemon juice; toss slightly. Blend Miracle Whip, sour cream, onion, and American cheese, and carefully fold into mixture. Season and place in well-buttered casserole dish. Top with Swiss cheese, and sprinkle buttered crumbs over cheese. Bake for about 30 minutes. Sometimes, if Roxie had leftover macaroni, she would put down a layer of it before the Swiss cheese.

To eat it cold, place leftovers between two slices of homemade bread with lettuce and tomato. I like to add chopped serranos and ranch dressing.

❧ BREAKFASTS ❧

EVERY MORNING Roxie would get up and make a good breakfast for my grandfather and us kids when we were staying with her. She made everything from fried eggs and bacon to venison sausage. One of my favorite things was her biscuits and gravy, with little bits of sausage that she and my aunts, Mini and Lois, made from scratch.

While Aunt Mini, Aunt Lois, and Roxie made sausages, they would have me sit under the table and watch them. First, they started grinding up the meat in the kitchen and then added all sorts of seasonings. The whole time, they would tell stories and give ideas on how they were going to do the sausage that year.

They used the wood-fired stove to heat up the skillet, and as they made the little sausage patties, I remember hearing a rhythm from their hands patting the meat. *Pat, pat, pat. Pat, pat.* They would throw a patty on the skillet and cook it to sample it for flavor. Together, they would determine if it needed more salt or something else. Lois might say it needed a little more salt. Then they would reevaluate, and Roxie might say it needed more pepper. But invariably, Aunt Mini would say, "It needs more sage." When it came to more sage in her sausage, Aunt Mini was as constant as the Northern Star. My job was to eat the leftover samples as the cooks perfected their recipe. It was a hard job, but I became quite adept.

Once they got the meat the way they finally wanted it, they stuffed it all into muslin tubes and placed them in the smoker to cure until rock hard. You could practically drive nails with them. To serve, they cut slices, fried them in lard or bacon drippings, and ate them as breakfast sausages.

I wish I had their exact recipe, but everything I've tried just doesn't come out the same as I remember. Instead, I leave you with the memory, and hope that one day you can find a breakfast sausage that lives up to it.

Smoking a Pig

Behind the house at Roxie's was a smokehouse. They smoked things over pecan wood and corncobs. When they slaughtered a hog, they hung the meat just beside the smokehouse and butchered it. I always knew they were planning to butcher a pig within days when I saw my aunts and Roxie bring in sheets of muslin and cut and sew them into long tubes for making sausage.

My uncles and cousins would show up around sunrise on the appointed day, and the first thing I saw at dawn was the smoke from their hand-rolled cigarettes and the steam from their coffee cups. Then I saw the sparks and initial smoke from the fires they had started for the smokehouse and the large cast-iron pot they used to scald the slaughtered pig.

When the family gathered to butcher a hog, it was a whole day affair, with a lot of effort and hard work. Breakfast at Roxie's usually wasn't very good on that day. I was a small kid, and they would make me stay inside because, they said, I was always "underfoot" and they were afraid I'd fall in the fire or play in the water.

They fed the pig special food for a while before slaughter to fatten it up and add more flavor to the meat. They prepared all sorts of cuts to smoke, like bacon and ham bone. They also used a lot of the cuts to grind and make sausage. On the day of butchering, Roxie and my aunts would sit in the warm kitchen and, using the muslin casings, make sausage from scratch.

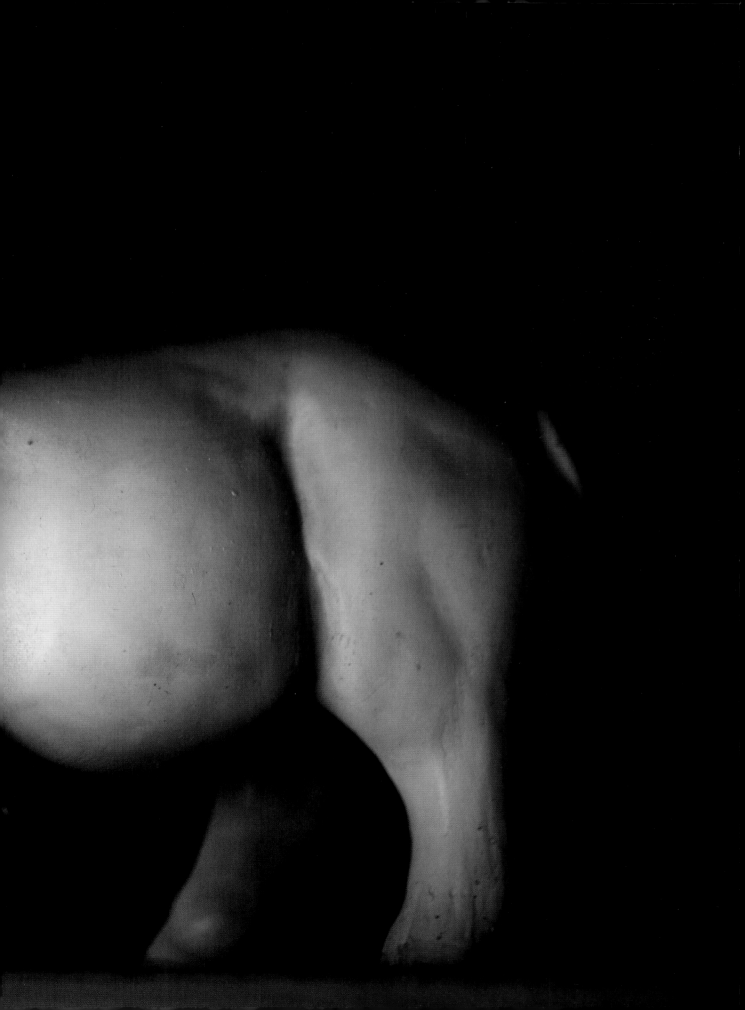

 DESSERTS

FRUIT AMBROSIA

WHEN I WAS young, my father got me all dressed up and put on his suit and we went down to my grandparents' house to a big party they were hosting. It turned out it was their golden wedding anniversary. There were maybe 50 or 60 people there. I remember surveying the table of food my grandmother had set out and fixing my eyes on a large cut-glass bowl filled with creamy white salad with pineapples and cherries and shredded coconut. It was the first time I'd ever seen Ambrosia salad. I helped myself to a serving and was taken with the sweet and creamy flavors and textures. Roxie would never tell her friends what her secret ingredient was, even though they always asked her. But I figured it out. One time, I saw an empty bottle of it in the trash bin: Kirschwasser, a German cherry liquor.

This salad isn't exactly the biggest gourmet achievement in America's culinary history, but I'll never forget discovering my first Ambrosia salad at my grandmother's golden wedding anniversary party.

The White House Cook Book *was one of Roxie's regular cooking resources. Her particular copy was printed in 1907.*

1 cup chopped apples
1 cup chopped oranges
1 can mandarin oranges, drained
2 cups sliced bananas
1 cup seeded and halved grapes
1 cup segmented and chopped grapefruit
1 cup halved cherries, drained
1 can pineapple, drained
2 teaspoons lemon juice
1 teaspoon lime juice
1 teaspoon almond extract
1 teaspoon vanilla extract
¼ cup Kirschwasser

16 ounces whipped cream
16 ounces sour cream
2 tablespoons powdered sugar, as needed
Shredded coconut
¼ cup toasted chopped pecans

Combine first 13 ingredients, cover, and refrigerate overnight. Mix in whipped cream and sour cream. Add powdered sugar as needed for binder. Place in serving bowl, and sprinkle top with shredded coconut and pecans. Garnish with more fruit, if desired. Chill and serve. Serves 12.

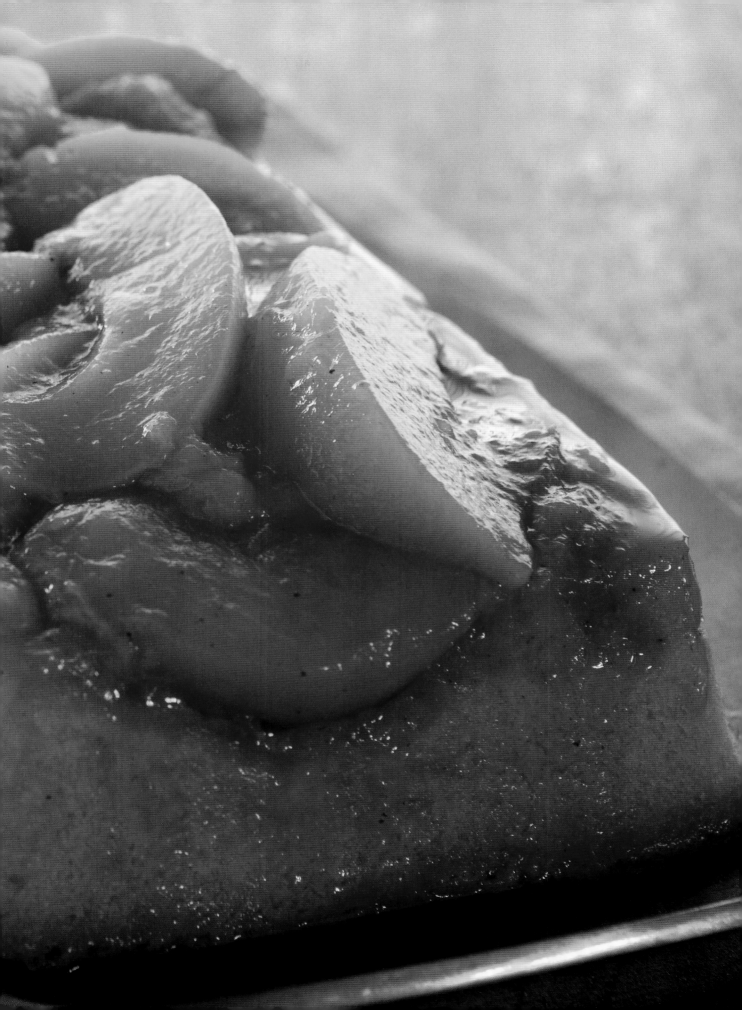

PEACH POUND CAKE

THE HILL COUNTRY OF TEXAS grows great peaches around the community of Stonewall, where LBJ had his ranch. In the summertime, we would travel up there and get some. We used peaches to make ice cream and cobblers in the summer, and we froze what we didn't immediately use with a little bit of sugar for the fall, when we would make pound cake and eat it warm.

Cake ingredients:
1 cup unsalted butter, plus more for pan
2 cups sifted cake flour (not self-rising)
½ teaspoon salt
2 peaches, in season, frozen, sliced
1½ cups sugar
⅓ cup puréed peaches (see recipe below)
5 large eggs, room temperature
2 teaspoons pure vanilla extract

Puréed peaches:
1 cup peaches, in season, frozen
¼ teaspoon cinnamon
½ teaspoon almond extract

Place peaches in blender and purée.

Preheat oven to 325 degrees. Lightly butter a 9 x 5–inch baking pan; place on a parchment-lined baking sheet. Set aside. Sift together flour and salt. Set aside. In bottom of well-buttered pan, arrange 10 to 12 peach slices.

Beat 1 cup butter with an electric mixer until fluffy. Gradually add sugar and ¼ cup peach puree until mixture is creamy. Add eggs, 1 at a time, beating well after each addition. Add vanilla. Gently fold in flour mixture cup by cup, blending after each addition; pour into pan.

Bake until cake springs back when touched, about 1½ hours. Let cake cool for 10 minutes, then turn onto wire rack.

DEWBERRY COBBLER

MY FAVORITE addition to the Sunday meal came in the spring, when dewberries were in season, because Roxie would make her famous dewberry cobbler, a recipe she had learned while growing up in the kitchen with my great grandmother, Bettie Howard, "Mammie." My Uncle Lum was Roxie's favorite brother. She always went out of her way to do special things for him. The dewberry cobbler was his absolute favorite treat. As soon as the dewberries began growing and ripening on the fences, she would pick them and invite him over for dinner. Uncle Lum had to drive a long way to get out to Roxie's house, but he always made the trip once a year for the dewberry cobbler.

I'll never forget the time my brother, Butch, and I shortchanged the entire family on dewberry cobbler. I was only about 5, and Uncle Lum (short for Christopher Columbus, a name Mammie gave him after the historic explorer) came to visit. I remember him being one of the tallest people I'd ever met. He seemed to tower over everyone in the family, except for Uncle Iverson. Something about him made me think he was Davy Crockett. Uncle Lum loved Roxie's Sunday dinners, and like I was, he was particularly fond of the dewberry cobbler.

The family all sat down to eat, and Butch and I tore through our dinner plates, piled high with fried chicken, green beans, and mashed potatoes with gravy. But as adults are wont to do, they ate their dinner more leisurely, discussing family history and local stories along the way. Not being able to wait another second for the prized cobbler, my brother and I snuck off to the kitchen to steal a bite of the sweet and buttery treat. Somehow one bite led to another. And another. And before we knew it, the cobbler was gone. By the time Roxie came in to retrieve the dessert for the family, we two boys had cleaned the edge of the pan with our sticky little fingers.

Though the entire family was disappointed by our gluttony, Uncle Lum was particularly upset. I later found out that was the first time in 20 years he had missed out on Roxie's homemade dewberry cobbler. The memory stuck with him. The next year that he visited for Roxie's Sunday dinner with dewberry cobbler, he made a special request, one that began a long tradition of Sunday dinners at Roxie's: We ate dessert first.

Because you can't really find dewberries much anymore, we're giving you the Salt Lick blackberry cobbler recipe. See page 242 for complete recipe.

Roxie was committed to rainwater collection. Not so much because it was sustainable, but because she swore that rainwater for cooking and washing her hair was far better than well water.

Beyond these stone
columns was a field
my grandpareants
used to raise
turkeys. Today the
only thing beyond
these columns are
beautiful Texas
sunsets.

CHAPTER THREE

HISAKO'S HOUSE

★ ★ ★

MY MOTHER wasn't from around here. She was from Hawaii; her parents, from Japan. When my father served in the Navy in World War II, he was stationed in Kauai. That's where he met Hisako Tsuchiyama, on the porch of a grocery store, and fell in love. Her sister, whom we called Aunt Tommie, was a translator for General MacArthur and went to Japan in his company. But Hisako didn't have her sights on the country of her heritage. She wanted to go to the mainland—especially after she met my father, Thurman. They fell in love and married.

Thurman knew he wanted to plant his roots back home in Driftwood, so he brought Hisako there to start a life together. She had a master's degree in psychology from UCLA, but she never took her education or career beyond that. Once she married my father, she devoted herself to building a life with him in Texas and starting a family. Bringing a Japanese wife home to Texas in the 1940s was a bit controversial, but it didn't seem to bother my parents. Driftwood was small then, and whatever negative thoughts people had did nothing to change their plans to start their family together.

My father's bridge construction work kept him on the road most of the time. Once we moved to Driftwood, my mother often went with him during the week while he worked on projects. That's how I came to spend so much time with my grandmother, Roxie. I don't have specific memories of my mother in the same way I do Roxie. My mother was usually very serious, she was very hardworking, and she was a perfectionist. She also had a knack for keeping everything to reuse—I think they call that recycling these days. In many ways, she was an environmentalist before her time. She kept everything: pickle jars for pickling watermelon rinds or cantaloupe, plastic bread bags to wrap up to-go orders at the restaurant, and cardboard boxes to package up large to-go orders. And paper egg cartons? She used those as kindling for the pit fires at the Salt Lick.

She was extremely supportive of my father. She was always thinking of ways to help him be successful at whatever he was doing, whether it was in the bridge-building business, in the pecan-shelling business he began in Driftwood in the mid-sixties, or in the barbecue restaurant. She was industrious and found a use for just about everything. Nothing went to waste.

When I think back, it seems all I remember my mother and father doing is working. Whether it was on our property, at the restaurant, in the garden, in the kitchen, Hisako was always doing something productive. It was just her way. One time she told me, "I'm really sorry that we didn't hug you a lot or that we weren't very encouraging in your childhood, but we were just not those kind of people." It's not the most nurturing acknowledgment to get from your mother, but I know that she was saying she loved me, even if she and my father didn't show it like many other parents do.

It didn't really make a difference to me growing up. That's all I knew. My parents worked. And they taught me to work. It never meant or felt like they loved me any less than anyone else I knew. It was just the way it was.

Though the food we serve at the Salt Lick is barbecue, my mother, just like family members in the generations before her, added a little something of her own to the menu. To enhance dishes such as our coleslaw and potato salad, she added popped sesame seeds, a flavor she grew up enjoying as a child in Hawaii. There was a time on Thursday nights that my dad would cook steaks at the restaurant. She would add her touch by making tempura-fried shrimp along with chrysanthemum petals and all sorts of vegetables from our garden. Zucchini squash, sweet potato, onion, parsley, green beans—she would tempura just about anything that was in season.

After my father passed away, in 1981, my mother continued to run the restaurant. I had a job in Austin, but I would come up on the weekends to help her out. It wasn't until 1987 that she retired and let me run everything. Of course, she never really let go of the business. She was always keeping an eye on things. She lived just down the road, so it was easy for her to check in. She would pop in daily and share her "wisdom" about what we were doing wrong. (She has shared a lot of that wisdom over the past several years.) For so much of her life with my father, the restaurant was all she had, so it was hard for her to just let go. She still visits and she still shares but not as much as she used to.

My mother's greatest gift for expressing love always showed through in the kitchen. She clipped and saved recipes from magazines and books and often tested them out on us. Some were failures and some were successes. But her soul came through in every one.

When cooking for us, she made all sorts of dishes. Some things were Southern, like chicken-fried steak and venison chili. But more than that, she also looked to what we had in our gardens. She would use those ingredients and adapt them with flavors from her heritage. Instead of Southern-style black-eyed peas, she used them in a stir fry. Instead of serving chicken-fried steak with mashed potatoes and gravy, she served it with white rice. She swore Texas had some of the best rice in the world and didn't want to mess up a dish with plain old potatoes if she could use rice instead.

In fact, there was a time when visitors from Japan would show up at our house. I didn't understand why they were there, but I later found out that they had come all the way over from Japan for Texas rice. Some of them said it was the second best rice in the world, compared to Japanese rice. And I remember one man said he thought the Texas rice was just as good if not better than Japanese rice—though I doubt that he'd go on record with that, even if I could find him. My mother would play host to the visitors so they could get their bearings in Texas before they headed down to the Victoria area to taste Texas rice.

In a lot of ways, Hisako was one of the first fusion-style cooks in Texas. She was about 50 years ahead of her time. She and my dad sold their produce and some confections that she made to area grocery stores. She sold fresh fruits and vegetables as well as jams made from figs, dewberries, blackberries, and wild mustang grapes. She even made pralines to sell, in all sorts of flavors—regular brown sugar, lemon, cinnamon. That was when we had the pecan-shelling and spice business. We imported all sorts of spices and distributed them to grocers and restaurants. We also shelled pecans by the ton and sold them. In our largest production year, we shelled more than 250,000 pounds of pecans.

WATERCRESS SALAD

WHEN I WAS YOUNG, I spent hours after school wandering the property and playing down by Onion Creek. One day, I came home with a few weeds from the riverbank stuck to my clothes. Hisako grabbed them off me and told me to go back to the creek and get a whole bunch more. I didn't understand why she wanted a whole bunch of weeds, but when I got back with a big handful of them, I soon found out why. It turns out they were wild watercress that grew in abundance down by the creek. She would fry up a little bacon, use the drippings to combine with a special dressing—that always had a lot of pepper—and pour it over the watercress with crumbled bacon. The leaves wilted from the warmth of the dressing. It was one of the best salads she made.

    6 large slices of smoked bacon
    2 tablespoons bacon grease
    1 tablespoon minced shallot
    1 teaspoon sugar
    3 tablespoons vinegar
    ½ teaspoon salt
    ¼ teaspoon white pepper
    4 bunches (12 ounces) cleaned watercress, excess stems removed

In a 10-inch skillet over medium to low heat, fry bacon until crispy. Place on paper towels to drain, then crumble. Reserve for topping salad. Reserve bacon grease from pan. Do not clean pan, and return 2 tablespoons grease to pan. Place over low heat, add shallots, and cook until translucent. While continuously stirring, add sugar, vinegar, salt, and pepper. Combine well, raise temperature to medium high, and continue stirring until mixture is hot enough to wilt watercress.

Divide watercress among 4 serving plates. Pour dressing mixture over greens and sprinkle with crumbled bacon. Serve immediately.

MY MOTHER HAD a number of go-to dishes that she would make for us during the week. She loved to test out different recipes that she would clip out from magazines and newspapers. And she always referred to her Betty Crocker cookbook as a resource for everything from basic bread to casseroles and cakes. Chief among her concerns was to use anything and everything she had in the kitchen. She wouldn't let anything go to waste. Sometimes that turned out in our favor, like when she would put bits of the spare ribs from the Salt Lick into her Portuguese soup. Other times, it wasn't so good. But the one thing that was certain was knowing that each evening, after I'd come home after a long, bumpy ride on the school bus, she'd have supper already in the works. These are some of my favorite dishes that she used to make.

CHICKEN-FRIED STEAK WITH RICE AND GRAVY

INSTEAD OF mashed potatoes, Hisako always served chicken-fried steak with rice. In her opinion, the rice in Texas was some of the best in the world. We have even had Japanese tourists come to visit the Salt Lick and then head straight for places like Victoria and Wharton to buy Texas rice to bring home to Japan. Although it's not an authentically Southern meal, her chicken-fried steak, rice, and gravy was pretty hard to beat. The secret to this dish is to drag the meat in flour on both sides before tenderizing it. Coat it lightly in flour, shake off the excess, put it on a hard surface, and pound the meat to tenderize it. The flour adheres to the meat and helps hold in moisture.

Seasoning mix:
1 teaspoon white pepper
1 tablespoon garlic salt

Lard
2 tablespoons bacon grease
2 cups flour
1 egg, lightly beaten
½ cup milk or buttermilk
8 6-ounce eye of round steaks
Salt and pepper to taste

Combine pepper and garlic salt for seasoning mix. Fill cast-iron skillet halfway with melted lard. Add bacon grease, and heat to 370 degrees. Mix flour with ½ teaspoon seasoning mix in large shallow bowl. In another shallow bowl whisk together egg and milk.

Moderately to heavily season steak with seasoning mix, dredge in flour on both sides, and tenderize with wooden meat mallet. Season and dredge before tenderizing to seal in flavors.

Dredge tenderized steaks in flour. Shake off excess. Dip into milk mixture, allowing excess to drop off, then dredge again in flour, evenly coating batter so that steak appears dry on the outside.

Gently place 2 to 3 steaks in oil. Oil temperature will fall, but maintain it at 325 degrees to 350 degrees. Cook steaks 7 minutes, turning twice, until batter is crisp and brown and meat is cooked through. Use wire skimmer or slotted spoon to transfer to plated paper towels. Season with salt and pepper to taste. Keep warm in oven. Serve with short grain white rice and cream gravy made in the same pan used to fry steaks. *NOTE: You can use leftover seasoning mix to flavor Cream Gravy (see page 42) or use Roxie's Pan Gravy recipe on page 33.*

A number of types of rice are available to cook with. Hisako always preferred short grain rice.

The Japanese-Texas Rice Connection

The Texas rice industry owes its origins to the introduction of rice seed from Madagascar to the Carolina colonies about 1685. Production, milling, and marketing flourished in South Carolina and Georgia for the next 200 years. Although there was early domestic cultivation of rice in Louisiana and Texas, commercial rice production began in Louisiana shortly before the Civil War and, in the 1880s, spread rapidly through the coastal prairies of southwest Louisiana into southeast Texas. Arkansas, California, Louisiana, and Texas now produce 90 percent of the American rice crop.

Considerable acreages of rice were grown in southeast Texas as early as 1853 by William Goyens and in Beaumont in 1863 by David French. The latter is often considered the first major rice farmer in Texas. Modern commercial production in Texas derived largely from the completion of the southern transcontinental railroad, in 1883, and its acquisition by the Southern Pacific Railroad, in 1885, coupled with the availability of cheap land on the coastal prairies, the introduction of modern rice mills, and an influx of immigrants from Louisiana and the grain-producing areas of the Midwest.

In 1891 Joseph E. Broussard established the first rice irrigation and canal system in the state, and the following year he added rice-milling machinery to an existing gristmill, thus initiating rice milling in Texas and paving the way for the rapid expansion of production. Texas farmers planted 234,000 acres of rice in 1903, compared to Louisiana's 376,000 acres. The two states then produced 99 percent of the total rice crop, with production having virtually ceased in South Carolina and Georgia.

An important event in the development of the Texas Gulf Coast rice industry was the introduction of seed imported from Japan in 1904. Seed rice had previously come from Honduras or the Carolinas. At the invitation of the Houston Chamber of Commerce and the Southern Pacific Railroad, Japanese farmers came to Texas to advise farmers on rice production, bringing with them seed as a gift from the emperor of Japan. The first three years' harvest, which produced an average of 34 barrels an acre compared with an average of 18 to 20 barrels from native rice seed, was sold as seed to Louisiana and Texas farmers. Japanese rice production began at Webster in Harris County under the direction of Seito Saibara, his family, and 30 original colonists. The Saibara family has been credited with establishing the Gulf Coast rice industry.

In Texas rice mills operated in Port Arthur, Beaumont, Orange, and Houston. Texas-milled rice went to world markets by rail and through the ports of Houston and Galveston.

Rice farming in the United States has historically been a large-scale capital-intensive enterprise, heavily dependent upon international markets. The United States markets annually 15 to 30 percent of the total world rice exports, although it accounts for only 2 percent of world production. Texas growers annually produce 20 million hundredweight of rice on 350,000 acres of land.

Excerpted from Henry C. Dethloff, "Rice Culture," Handbook of Texas Online (www.tshaonline.org/handbook/online/articles/afr01), accessed January 11, 2012. Published by the Texas State Historical Association.

CHICKEN-FRIED VENISON

ONE AUTUMN, my mother went down to a little grove on our property to collect pecans. She used the detergent All to do our laundry and always saved the metal pails it came in to collect pecans. That particular day was during deer season, and my father was hosting friends for one of his big hunts on the property. While my mother was picking up pecans, a big buck came running down the hillside, right at her. She was so alarmed that in self-defense she swung the bucket full of pecans and hit the deer in the antlers. Shocked from the blow, the deer fell to the ground. She then grabbed a large rock and ended the intruder's life.

When we all got back from hunting, none of us had bagged anything. But here was my little Japanese mother, asking us if we would go down the hill to get the deer she killed with an All pail. She was more upset that she dumped her whole bucket of pecans than impressed by her ability to take down a deer without a firearm.

Most people use venison backstrap, but my mother used meat from the whole deer. See recipe on opposite page for Chicken-Fried Steak for instructions.

CHICKEN-FRIED STEAK
WITH RICE AND GRAVY

BLACK-EYED PEAS

MY GRANDMOTHER had a way of making fresh black-eyed peas taste divine. But her recipe was more of a Southern take on field peas. Hisako liked to use fresh black-eyed peas as well, but she would pick them before they were too ripe, leave them in their hulls, and stir-fry them in peanut oil with bits of pork, garlic, and a little bit of ginger and soy.

½ pound pork loin or pork shoulder, if you prefer a little more fat

Marinade:
2 teaspoons sake, or mirin
1 tablespoon soy
½ teaspoon sugar
¼ teaspoon salt
½ teaspoon minced fresh ginger

Cut pork loin into ¼-inch pieces. Combine ingredients for marinade, and add pork. Set aside for at least 1 hour.

Ingredients:
5 cups young black-eyed peas, in the shell
1½ tablespoon cornstarch
1 cup chicken stock
1 tablespoon soy
1 teaspoon sugar
½ teaspoon salt
2 tablespoons peanut oil

In a large pot of water parboil peas, then blanch in an ice bath for 1 minute. Remove and set aside. In a small saucepot over medium heat, combine cornstarch, chicken stock, soy, sugar, and salt, and stir constantly to form gravy.

Heat peanut oil in a large frying pan. Add pork, and sauté until brown. Stir in black-eyed peas. Add gravy and bring to boil. Remove from fire, and serve immediately with short grain white rice.

Traditional southern-style black-eyed peas simmered with pork and onions are a classic favorite. But Hisako's stir-fried fresh black-eyed peas will always stand out as a new way to enjoy them.

LAMB CHOPS

FOR A WHILE we raised sheep on the ranch. We had about 250 in a given year. When it was time to shear their coats, a bunch of workers would come in and get them all in order. There was a large barn on our property, with a big pen where we held the sheep. (The barn was later torn down and used to build the first part of the Salt Lick restaurant.) A long narrow chute ran off one side of the pen through which the workers funneled one sheep at a time for shearing.

One day, my mother was helping out and stood at a hole in the large pen to hold the sheep inside while one of our crew was getting wire to mend it. But somehow one sheep broke through her hold, and just as sheep do, the rest of them followed. It was quite a force against my mother. She fell over, and the entire herd ran over her. She was trampled by stampeding sheep! She couldn't get out of bed for five days, and I don't think she ever helped with the sheep again.

In the spring we always had lamb. Hisako's secret was to flavor the oil with slices of garlic. She let them simmer in the oil at a low temperature until they were barely brown and then take them out. Turns out it was her secret to a lot of her meat dishes.

Hisako would often serve homemade mint jelly with her lamb chops. Today you can easily find decent versions of mint jelly in grocery stores, but you can always give a home-made recipe a try.

> 2 large garlic cloves, crushed
> 1 tablespoon fresh rosemary leaves
> 1 teaspoon fresh thyme leaves
> Pinch cayenne pepper
> 2 tablespoons extra-virgin olive oil
> 6 lamb chops, about ¾-inch thick
> Salt and pepper to taste
> 1 garlic clove, sliced

In a food processor fitted with a metal blade, add garlic, rosemary, thyme, and cayenne. Pulse until combined. Pour in olive oil, pulsing into paste. Rub paste on both sides of lamb chops, and marinate for at least 2 hours in the refrigerator. Remove chops from refrigerator and allow to come to room temperature, about 20 minutes. Wipe off some of the marinade, and season lamb with a little salt and pepper. *NOTE: We add salt at this time as opposed to during the marinating because that takes moisture from the meat. Our suggestion is to salt meat right when you intend to cook it.*

Add oil to a frying pan. Add slices of garlic and let sit over medium heat to flavor the oil. Do not let garlic burn. Remove garlic and discard. Heat pan over high heat until almost smoking, add chops, and sear for about 2 minutes. Flip the chops and cook for another 3 minutes for medium rare and 3½ minutes for medium.

ROXIE'S CHICKEN 'N DUMPLINGS

BOTH ROXIE and my mother made amazing Chicken 'n Dumplings. But my first experience with the dish was from my mom's recipe, which had really fluffy dumplings. Roxie's dumplings were more flat and dense. They were good, but they didn't look right to me. I'll never forget the look on her face when I told her she was making her dumplings wrong. Thinking back now, I'm lucky I ever had Sunday dinner at her house again.

Though their recipes were different, they did share the same secret, which is to start the day before so that you can remove the fat. In the South? Remove the fat? Yes, it is heresy, but it is true. Chicken and dumplings is just a better dish without the fat.

1 whole chicken, about 3 pounds
1 onion, chopped
8 cups water
¼ teaspoon garlic powder
¼ teaspoon black pepper
¼ teaspoon salt

Dumplings:
2 cups flour
1 teaspoon pepper
¾ cup ice water
¾ cup butter

In large pot over high heat, place chicken, onion, and water. Add more water to cover chicken if necessary. Bring to a boil, cover, and simmer for 2 hours, or until meat falls off bone. Strain the broth, reserving the chicken, return broth to pan, and refrigerate overnight. After chicken cools, remove meat from bone. Discard skin and bones. Cover chicken and refrigerate.

When ready to prepare the dish (after at least 1 day), skim solidified fat from broth and discard. Bring broth to a boil, add garlic powder, pepper, salt, and chicken meat to boiling broth, and return it to a simmer.

For dumplings, combine flour and pepper in a mound in mixing bowl. Drizzle a small amount of water into center of flour. Using fingers, gradually incorporate the water into the flour. Knead dough and form a ball. Roll out dough to ⅛-inch thickness and cut into 1-inch pieces. Let rest.

Cut pieces of dough in half and drop into simmering soup until all have been added. Turn broth in a circular motion so that dumplings submerge and cook. Do not stir. Cook until dumplings float, 3 to 4 minutes. Ladle chicken, gravy, and dumplings into warm bowls and serve.

ROXIE'S CHICKEN 'N DUMPLINGS

HISAKO'S CHICKEN 'N DUMPLINGS

HISAKO'S CHICKEN 'N DUMPLINGS

1 chicken, about 3½ pounds
8 cups water
3 large stalks celery, chopped
1 teaspoon thyme
1 bay leaf
1 onion, diced
2 carrots, sliced

The key to Hisako's chicken and dumplings was light and fluffy dumplings. She would gently place the dough over the chicken and gravy so they would puff up and cook without getting weighed down.

Place all ingredients into pot and add additional water to cover if necessary. Bring to a boil, cover, and simmer. Cook until chicken is firm and tender, thigh juices run clear, and vegetables are tender.

Strain broth into pot, cover, and refrigerate. Remove skin and bones from chicken and discard along with bay leaf. Cover and refrigerate chicken and vegetables.

When ready to prepare the dish (at least 24 hours later), skim fat from top of broth and discard. Place pot on burner, add back chicken and vegetables, bring to a boil, and reduce to a simmer.

Gravy:
¼ cup plus 2 tablespoons flour
¾ cup milk
¾ cup chicken broth
¼ teaspoon white pepper
¼ teaspoon garlic powder
¼ teaspoon salt
1 tablespoon butter

Place flour into a bowl, add ½ cup milk, and stir to make a batter with no lumps. Place ¾ cup broth and remaining milk into pot, and bring to a boil. Add remaining ingredients and simmer until thickened. Stir mixture into broth.

Dumplings:
2 cups flour
1 teaspoon salt
3 teaspoons baking powder
1 cup milk
3 tablespoons vegetable oil

This is the type of hat my father would wear all the time.

Combine flour, salt, and baking powder in bowl. Stir in milk and oil. Let rest a few minutes. Drop mixture from tablespoon into simmering gravy until surface is covered or dough is used. Dumplings slide off easy if you dip spoon in gravy each time. Cook uncovered, simmering for 5 minutes. Cover and cook for an additional 5 minutes. Ladle chicken and gravy into warm bowls, top with dumplings, and serve.

THURMAN LEE ROBERTS, SR.
27 October 1908 – 29 April 1981
U.S. NAVY

Thurman's Mansion

M Y FATHER was a hardworking man who was loyal to his family. He worked hard throughout his career in the Navy, as a bridge construction contractor, as a truck farmer, and as the owner of the Salt Lick. He never really took a vacation—except for one time. He had a fascination with the American gold rush and had always wanted to go to Alaska. So in 1970 he took my mother and me to Alaska for a month. At the time we were the only employees at the restaurant, so we had to close it while we were gone. He bought a big 4 x 8 piece of plywood and painted on it: "Tired. Gone to Alaska. Will reopen in September." Apparently someone really liked the sign and stole it while we were gone. When we got back, our business was nonexistent. Everyone thought we had closed down. It took about six months for people to realize we were still around. He didn't take any more vacations after that.

In the late 1970s, after the Salt Lick had been open for a good while, my father decided he wanted to build my mother a new home. We had a perfect spot at the top of a hill that overlooked the entire Driftwood valley. You can see for miles. I told him he should build a house there, and he agreed. He worked on the house for four years, crafting it with just a little help from his staff. He quarried rock from the property and used it to create the foundation and eight large concrete columns. He then started building rock walls and finally added the roof.

Late one afternoon he was walking through, inspecting the house, and he sat down on a windowsill, taking in the view. I don't know what he was thinking about, but my mother told me he was out there for a long time, maybe two or three hours. When he came home, it was night. He told my mother good night and went to sleep, but he never woke up.

The strange thing is that he had just been to the doctor for a checkup that very day and received a clean bill of health. The doctor told him he would probably even outlive him. To celebrate the good news, my mother had bought a lobster for dinner that night. But thinking it was too much of an extravagance for that evening, she ended up freezing it for another occasion. After he passed away in the night, she held on to so much guilt for not having made that special lobster dinner for him. It would have been his last meal.

The mansion my dad began stayed unfinished for more than 20 years. My mom was running the restaurant, and I was working in another career and taking care of my wife and daughter. Over the years, the mansion was vandalized and ignored. In 2005 I finally got it in my head that I needed to finish what my father had started. By that time I was running the restaurant and had expanded the business in a number of ways. We added an outside addition and completed the mansion within the year. The second floor houses our main offices. On the first floor we host special events, including weddings, private parties, and meetings. Though my dad never saw his great home completed, I know he would be proud of what it has become. Today I often stand out on the second story balcony just outside of my office and take in the view he once saw. Sometimes I wonder what he thought about on his last day here.

A few signature recipes remind me of my dad, aside from his barbecue. The first is a grilled steak that he soaked in a peach-brandy marinade. There was a time when he and my mother got tired of cooking only barbecue, so they had Thursday steak nights. He would do his special aged sirloin steaks on the grill. Hisako added tempura-fried shrimp and sweet onions to serve with the steaks.

For dessert, my father had a fondness for cherry pie. In fact, when I was looking back through old family recipes, I found a recipe titled Thurman's Sour Cream Cherry Pie. It wasn't something we served at the restaurant, but it is something he loved to indulge in from time to time.

Steak nights at the Salt Lick were a way for my parents to break from cooking barbecue. But it was also a way for Thurman to perfect steak. The only way to do that is to do it over and over again. As they say, "Practice makes perfect."

THURMAN'S STEAK WITH PEACH BRANDY

1 steak of your preference
1 tablespoon garlic salt
1 teaspoon white pepper
½ cup peach brandy and 1 tablespoon lime juice, combined

Season steak, and add a little score in meat with butcher's mallet. On hot grill, sear steak on both sides to create crust. Baste top of steak with brandy–lime juice mixture. Turn and cook until halfway done, according to your preference. (See sidebar on cooking a steak.) Baste other side while waiting for first side to cook, then flip and cook second side. *NOTE: The time will vary depending on cut of meat. Our suggestion is to cook steak to medium rare and let it rest.*

Remove steak from grill when done. Brush both sides once more with baste and let rest for at least 10-15 minutes depending on the thickness of the steak. (You want the hot juices to settle back into the meat.). When ready to serve, throw steak back on very hot grill for just 1 or 2 minutes to bring it back up to serving temperature. Serve immediately.

How to Know When Your Steak Is Done on the Grill

A lot of people get nervous about cooking a steak on the grill because they never quite know when their steak is done. The biggest thing to understand about cooking meat is that the heat tightens up all the muscle tissue, making the meat plump. As the fat in the meat begins to cook, the meat changes texture again and begins to relax. You can easily determine how far along your steak is simply by touching it with a spatula or fork. But whatever you do, DO NOT cut into the steak while it is cooking to see what color it is. Not only do you ruin the chemistry of steak cooking under heat but you also get an inaccurate doneness read based on color, because the juices are melted and flowing throughout the meat when it is hot anyway.

The best way to understand when a steak is done is to know what the texture of the steak feels like from start to finish. Take the raw steak and place it on a plate. With your spatula or fork, press down and move the spatula back and forth. Get a good feel for how the steak moves between the top and bottom.

- A well-done, or overcooked, steak will have almost no motion between top and bottom.
- A medium rare steak will have a little motion between top and bottom but will feel stiffer.

This is a skill that you have to practice. Remember that you can always put a steak back on the grill if it is too rare, but you cannot uncook a well-done steak. Err on the side of undercooked, and throw it back on the grill if you need to. If you pay attention to the way a steak cooks, you'll get better at telling when it is just perfect.

Finally, don't forget the last step in cooking meat: letting it rest. If you serve a steak immediately off the grill, all the juices seep out onto the plate and make everything wet. That also takes all of the flavor out. Instead, take the steak off the grill just before it reaches the doneness you would like. Let it rest for at least 15 minutes, and DO NOT cut it. That will allow the juices and fats to cool down and remain where they should be, in the meat. Once you have let the steak rest, you can quickly bring it back up to temperature in a very hot oven or on a very hot grill for just a couple of minutes before serving.

HISAKO'S SHRIMP TEMPURA

Canola oil for frying

⅔ cup sifted flour

3 tablespoons cornstarch

1 teaspoon baking powder

¼ teaspoon salt

1 egg, slightly beaten

½ to ¾ cup water

1½ pounds jumbo shrimp, cleaned and deveined

In a deep frying pan, heat oil to 350 degrees. Sift dry ingredients together twice. Add egg to ½ cup water. Add dry ingredients gradually. If too thick, add a little more water. Do not mix too thoroughly. Sprinkle a few drops of batter in oil to test heat. Repeat several times to create a "lacy" background. Then dip 3 or 4 shrimp in batter and place carefully on lacy batter. Sprinkle more batter on top of shrimp. After 1 minute, turn shrimp over to cook other side. Remove and drain on paper towels. Repeat until all shrimp are cooked. Serves 8.

HISAKO'S
SHRIMP
TEMPURA

GRILLED CORN
WITH COTIJA

THURMAN'S STEAK
WITH PEACH BRANDY

ROXIE'S WHITE BREAD

SAUTEED POTATOES

BAKED SWEET ONIONS

BAKED SWEET ONIONS

THE PREPARATION made a candy-like sweet onion that I, even as a child, loved. It was very nice to have a candy at dinner that counted as a vegetable. Try this recipe with Texas 1015 onions, and it will blow your skirt up.

½ cup vinegar

½ cup sugar

½ cup water

½ cup butter

2 tablespoons salt

4 medium to large onions (preferably 1015s), cleaned and peeled,
    with tops removed

Preheat oven to 325 to 350 degrees. In saucepot, boil together first 5 ingredients until sugar is dissolved. Arrange onions in casserole with 3-inch lip, cut-side up. Pour mixture over onions. Bake for 30 minutes or until onions are tender, occasionally basting while baking. Tops may brown, but that is desirable. If they are getting too brown on top but still not softened inside, cover with foil.

There's really nothing to fluting the edges of a pie crust. Using both hands, you just pinch your thumbs against your forefingers in opposite directions along the whole round of the dish. Try not to overwork the dough or it will get sticky. Give it a quick pinch and go.

THURMAN'S SOUR CREAM CHERRY PIE

1 cup milk

1 cup sour cream

1 cup sugar

½ teaspoon cinnamon

¼ teaspoon cloves

¼ cup flour

½ teaspoon vanilla

½ teaspoon almond extract

1 teaspoon lemon juice

1 can cherries

2 tablespoon flour

2 store-bought refrigerated pie crusts

Preheat oven to 350 degrees. Combine first 11 ingredients, pour into 9-inch pie crust. Cover the pie with second pie crust and carefully crimp the sides together. Use a fork to mark through the center of the top pie crust to allow air to escape. Bake 40 to 50 minutes. (*NOTE: For a prettier finish, brush the top of the pie with egg wash—one egg and a splash of water whisked together—and add a sprinkle of sugar.*)

Thurman was never able to see his finished vision of the house he was building for my mother. It wasn't until 2005 that the project he began in the early 1980s was finally completed.

❧ WEEKNIGHT MEALS ❧

HISAKO HAD a number of standby recipes for dinner during the week. They weren't anything special, but whenever I have some of those dishes, it brings me back to when I was young. I watched her make something delicious out of whatever we had on hand. While some home cooks suffer at making something out of nothing, Hisako could make just about anything taste good. She wasted nothing. These are a few of my favorite weeknight meals.

TAMALE PIE

THE BUS RIDE to grade school in Buda was an hour and a half long. That is a long 14-mile trip for an 8-year-old. It was so boring that when a full seat came available, I would lie down, close my eyes, and dream. After eight years, I had every curb and bump memorized, even in my closed-eye state. When I knew we were having Tamale Pie for supper, the trip became excruciating. Off the bus, running down the driveway, I could smell it halfway home. Then there it was, sitting all golden on the kitchen counter.

This is a typical casserole recipe, but I absolutely loved it. It was just one of those special things Hisako might serve on an average Tuesday night.

For filling:
½ cup vegetable oil
1 pound ground steak
1 medium onion, chopped
2 cloves garlic
1 teaspoon garlic salt
3 tablespoons butter
1 8-ounce can whole kernel corn and liquid
1 8-ounce can crushed tomatoes
2 teaspoons chile powder

For cornbread topping:
3 beaten eggs
¼ cup vegetable oil
1½ cups corn meal
1½ cups sweet milk, evaporated
1 teaspoon baking powder
½ teaspoon baking soda
1 tablespoon salt
2 teaspoons sugar

For filling: Preheat oven to 350 degrees. Combine first six ingredients in large skillet, and brown the meat. Add corn, tomatoes, and chile powder. Cook together for 15 minutes. Transfer ingredients to a casserole dish.

For cornbread topping: In a separate bowl, combine all ingredients. Pour over meat mixture, and bake 30 to 35 minutes or until the top has browned.

PORTUGUESE BEAN SOUP

MY MOTHER never let anything go to waste. She managed to use just about everything in our kitchen to make a meal. Sometimes she would hit a home run with some new concoction. Other times, it was a swing and a miss. But overall, she had a good palate and knew how to make things taste good together. This soup is a perfect example of how she would use just about everything but the kitchen sink to make something better. The first time, she made it to use up smoked sausage that we didn't sell at the restaurant over the weekend. We all liked the soup so much that she kept altering the recipe, using leftover meat from the restaurant. Usually it was sausage, but sometimes we would come upon a bone or two when she used leftover pork ribs. I don't think she ever used the brisket, but I know she never used chicken—my dad refused to add chicken to his barbecue menu.

¾ cup each dried pinto beans, garbanzo beans, and kidney beans
1 tablespoon olive oil or vegetable oil
3 cloves garlic, minced or pressed
1 medium onion, chopped
1 cup diced celery
2 quarts beef stock
1 ham hock
1 quart water
1 bay leaf
1 can (1 pound, 12 ounces) whole tomatoes
¾ pound cooked kielbasa, Polish, or smoked sausage
Salt and pepper to taste
Chopped fresh parsley
Grated Parmesan cheese

Wash beans, cover with water, and soak overnight. Before cooking, drain and add fresh water. Heat slowly to boiling. Meanwhile, heat oil in heavy soup kettle. Add garlic, onion, and celery, and sauté 2 to 3 minutes or until golden. Drain beans, and add to vegetable mixture. Add beef stock, ham hock, water, and bay leaf. Heat to simmering over low heat for 4 hours. Add tomatoes. Cut sausages into 1-inch lengths, and add to soup. Heat through. Season to taste. Serve with a sprinkling of fresh parsley and Parmesan cheese. Makes 6 to 8 servings.

SPLIT-PEA SOUP

I USED TO hate split-pea soup. My mother made it all the time, and I couldn't stand it. I think the color and the texture was what turned me off. But for some reason, my parents thought it was really good for me and would try to make me eat it. It was the great standoff. I would sit at the table, staring at that cold bowl of soup for at least two hours before they would finally give up and let me go.

But it's funny how age changes you. I remember later, as an adult, being at a dinner party where split-pea soup was served. I was talking to a friend and spooned a bite of it without knowing what it was. The rich ham hock flavors and the sweetness of the peas exploded in my mouth. It was delicious. Now this is one of my favorite soups to enjoy in the wintertime. *NOTE: For a Salt Lick variation, try this recipe with smoked turkey instead of ham. A few slices of serrano pepper give it an extra kick.*

2¼ cups dried split peas
2 quarts cold water
1½ pounds ham hock
2 onions, thinly sliced
½ teaspoon salt
¼ teaspoon ground black pepper
3 stalks celery, chopped
3 carrots, chopped
1 potato, diced

In a large stockpot, cover peas with water and soak overnight. (If you need a faster method, simmer the peas gently for 2 minutes, and then soak for 1 hour.) Discard soaking water and cover peas with fresh water in the stockpot. Add ham hock, onion, salt, and pepper. Cover, bring to boil, and simmer for 1½ hours, stirring occasionally. Remove bone, cut off meat, dice, and return meat to soup. Add vegetables. Cook slowly, uncovered, for 30 to 40 minutes, or until vegetables are tender. Serves 12.

It may be true that split-pea soup isn't the prettiest of classic soups, but it certainly is one of the most delicious. It took me long into my adulthood to know that, but the sweetness from the peas balanced by the savoriness of the ham hock is the perfect marriage of flavors.

1968 GREEN MUSTANG GRAPE PRESERVES

MUSTANG GRAPES grow wild around Driftwood. They are delicious to eat if you pick them at just the right time. My mother taught us how to check the grapes when they came into season. It had to be early in the season, when the grapes were still green, before the seeds began to form in the fruit. When that small window opened, everything on the ranch stopped. She enlisted all of us to scour the few places around Onion Creek where they grew and bring back sacks and sacks of them. She had big pots set up and added the grapes. As they cooked in water, they reached a point where the skins turned from green to purple and the result would be a dark, almost black sauce. It was more of a tart style of preserve, but it was absolutely delicious. She primarily made the preserves for breakfast toast and biscuits. But one of us used it on vanilla ice cream once at the restaurant, and it was a match made in heaven. In fact, it became one of the best-selling desserts for us.

    3 quarts mustang grapes
    1 five-pound bag of sugar

Wash grapes and remove stems. Bring 1 pint water to a boil. Add sugar and dissolve to make a syrup. Add grapes and bring to a rolling boil, then reduce heat to medium-high and cook slowly until most of the water evaporates and the skins begin to pop. Seal in glass jars. Yields approximately 10 half-pint jars.

FIG PRESERVES

MY MOTHER had a garden on the side of our house with a big fig tree in the corner. I used to play in the garden a lot and help her pull weeds. I remember, when the figs were in season, she went out each day to check on which ones were just right for picking. Once she had a good collection, she used them for all sorts of recipes. And when she couldn't think of anything else to use them in, she made fig preserves. When she made preserves, the fruit was the real star. She didn't make things too sweet. The main fruit ingredient really stood out.

    3 pounds figs, peeled and quartered lengthwise
    2 cups sugar
    Juice and zest of 1 lemon

In a large saucepan, combine figs, sugar, juice, and zest. Simmer over medium low heat, stirring constantly. Cover and simmer over low heat for 1 hour. Uncover and continue to simmer, stirring constantly until mixture thickens.

While figs are cooking, prepare the jars and lids. Put the glass jars in a boiling water canner half-filled with water. Bring to a boil; reduce heat and keep jars in the water. Simmer water in a saucepan, reduce heat to low, and add jar lids. Keep in the hot water until ready to use. Do not boil.

Fill jars with hot fig jam, leaving ½-inch headspace. Wipe jar rims and threads well. Place lids on jars using tongs or jar magnet, then screw on the rings. Place on rack in the hot water in the canner. Lower into the water and add enough hot or boiling water to bring the water level 1 to 2 inches above the jars. Bring to a boil for 10 minutes. Yields 4 half-pint jars.

❧ PICKLES ❧

MY MOTHER made pickles out of just about everything. I've included recipes for some of my favorites, including her watermelon rind pickles. These are a rare find these days but worth the effort.

WATERMELON PICKLES

Watermelon

Brine:
6 cups water
5 teaspoons salt

Syrup:
1⅓ cups sugar
1 tablespoon salt
1 cup white vinegar
3 cups water

Spice bag:
5 ¼-inch slices fresh ginger
5 whole cloves
5 whole allspice berries
1 cinnamon stick
Cheesecloth for spice bag

Peel outer green layer from rind. (Reserve flesh for eating, making agua fresca, or another use.) Leave about a ¼-inch thick of the red flesh on the rind. Cut rind into pieces that are ½ inch thick, ½ inch wide, and 2 inches long. Bring brine to a boil in large saucepan over medium high heat. Add rind to pan, reduce heat and simmer 15 minutes until crisp-tender. Drain rind and place in large bowl. Discard brine. For syrup, dissolve sugar and salt in saucepan with vinegar and water. For spice bag, gather cheesecloth around spices, tie securely, and drop into syrup. Boil until sugar and salt are dissolved. Pour spiced syrup over rind.

Cover and chill for 12 hours. If canning, distribute rind into 5 pint jars, place 1 clove, 1 allspice berry, and 1 ginger slice into each jar, and pour syrup into each jar until it reaches 1 inch below the top. Seal and submerge in boiling water for 10 to 15 minutes. Chill at least 8 hours before serving.

CANTALOUPE PICKLES

Brine:

1 cup salt

1 gallon water

Overnight soaking liquid:

2 quarts water

4 cups sugar

Spiced pickling juice:

2 cups vinegar

2 cups sugar

1 stick cinnamon

1 tablespoon whole cloves

1 tablespoon whole allspice

1 slice ginger root, ¼ inch thick, julienned into 4 slices

Remove rind and seed from cantaloupe. Cut into uniform 1-inch pieces. Dissolve salt in water, soak cantaloupe in brine for 3 hours, and drain. Boil 2 quarts water with 4 cups sugar for about 5 minutes. Add cantaloupe, and boil for 30 minutes. Turn off heat and let stand 6 hours or overnight. Combine ingredients for spiced pickling juice, add to syrup and melon, and cook until melon is translucent. (If syrup becomes too thick, stir in boiled water.) Pack melon into hot jars, distributing spiced syrup evenly into each jar, and fill with liquid to 1 inch below the top of the jar. Seal and submerge in hot water for 10 to 15 minutes. Remove and cool.

BEET PICKLES

6 pounds fresh small beets, whole, or large beets cut into 2-inch cubes

3 cups beet water

5 1-pint jars

2 tablespoons whole cloves

1 cup white sugar

2 cups white vinegar

1½ teaspoons pickling salt

Place beets in large stockpot with water to cover. Bring to a boil, and cook until tender, about 15 minutes. Strain, reserving 3 cups of beet water, cool, and peel. Sterilize jars and lids by immersing in boiling water for at least 10 minutes. Fill each jar with beets and add several whole cloves to each jar. In a large saucepan, combine the sugar, beet water, vinegar, and pickling salt. Bring to a rapid boil. Pour hot brine over beets in jars, and seal lids. Place a rack in the bottom of a large stockpot and fill halfway with water. Bring to a boil over high heat, then carefully lower jars into the pot using a holder. Leave a 2-inch space between jars. Pour in more boiling water if necessary until the water level is at least 1 inch above the tops of the jars. Bring the water to a full boil, cover the pot, and process for 10 minutes.

JALAPEÑO PICKLES

4 pounds jalapeños, unblemished; smaller ones are better
9 carrots, sliced into ¼-inch pieces on the bias
4 to 5 onions, sliced in ¼-inch strips

6 cloves garlic, 1 clove per jar, each sliced in thirds
6 teaspoons whole black peppercorns, 1 teaspoon per jar

Brine:
3 quarts water
1 cup kosher salt
1 quart white vinegar
1 dried whole chile pepper

Wash and prepare vegetables. Drop garlic cloves and peppercorns into each jar. Layer carrots, onions, then jalapeños. For the brine, boil all ingredients until salt dissolves. Remove chile pepper. Pour brine evenly into each jar to 1 inch below the top. Refrigerate or proceed with canning by sealing each jar and submerging into hot water for 10 to 15 minutes. Cool. When ready to serve, Hisako recommends pouring a little salad oil into the jars, which will add luster to the jalapeños as they are removed.

My mother collected all sorts of cookbooks, from the classic Betty Crocker's Picture Cook Book *to books that focused on recipes from Hawaii, where she grew up. But she always made her own corrections in the margins to the recipes she used most.*

❧ BREAKFAST AND DESSERTS ❧

I TALKED ABOUT how hot the summers would get when growing up in Driftwood, especially since we didn't have air-conditioning. We didn't have heating either. So when it was hot, it was really hot. And when it was cold, it was really cold. In the winter, when I'd wake up sometimes in the morning the room would be so cold that I could see the vapors of my breath. On some of those mornings, Hisako would have already been up and she would be making French toast, cinnamon toast, fresh pastries, or fresh blueberry muffins. The smell of her baking was the only thing that could get me out from under the warm covers on one of those cold winter mornings.

BLUEBERRY MUFFINS

WHEN BLUEBERRIES came into season, my parents would go to Hyden Grocery Store on South Lamar in Austin and buy a whole wooden crate of them. Mom would freeze most of them for later use, but for about a week every morning we ate wonderful yellow muffins filled with blueberries. They would come out of the oven hot and soak up all the butter I could put on them.

    2 cups all-purpose flour
    1 cup sugar
    ½ teaspoon salt
    1 tablespoon double-acting baking powder
    2 eggs
    1 cup milk
    ¼ cup vegetable oil
    1 cup blueberries, frozen is okay
    3 tablespoons flour, for dusting blueberries

Grease 12-muffin pan with 2½-inch cups. Preheat oven to 400 degrees. Mix flour, sugar, salt, and baking powder with a fork in a large bowl. In another large bowl, beat egg slightly then stir in milk and oil.

All at once, add egg mixture to flour mixture, and stir until just moistened. Then coat blueberries with flour and gently fold into batter. That will prevent the blueberries from falling to the bottom of the muffin. *NOTE: Over-mixing causes toughness; batter should be lumpy.* Spoon batter into muffin pan, wiping up any spills.

Bake muffins 20 to 25 minutes, until they are well risen and golden and a toothpick placed into a muffin center comes out clean and dry.

You can always use frozen blueberries for this recipe if fresh ones aren't in season. But when they are in season, you'll be able to taste the delicious difference.

GINGERBREAD WITH LEMON SAUCE

THIS WAS a classic dessert my mom would make. It's not an unusual recipe, but gingerbread in particular is something sentimental to me. It is not just because my mom made it for us while we were growing up. It was also the first recipe my daughter, Maile, made in a kids' cooking class. She was in summer camp at Hill Country Middle School in Austin, one of the few schools that had a home economics kitchen. One day, the class made a fresh batch of gingerbread, and she proudly brought it home for my wife, Susan, and me. I'll never forget how excited she was to have baked something on her own. I liked my mother's gingerbread a lot, but I think Maile's first batch was the best I've ever had.

½ cup sugar
½ cup shortening
1 egg
½ cup molasses
1½ cups flour
¾ teaspoon salt
¾ teaspoon soda
½ teaspoon cinnamon
¾ teaspoon ginger
½ cup boiling water

Preheat oven to 350 degrees, and grease an 8 x 8 x 2–inch pan. Gradually cream sugar into shortening in large mixer bowl until light and fluffy. Add egg and molasses, and beat thoroughly. In a separate bowl, stir together dry ingredients. Add to molasses mixture, alternating with boiling water, beating well after each addition. Bake for about 34 minutes or until a toothpick comes out clean.

Lemon sauce:
½ cup sugar
2 teaspoons cornstarch
½ teaspoon salt
1 cup cold water
2 egg yolks, lightly beaten
2 tablespoons butter
1 teaspoon lemon zest
3 tablespoons lemon juice
Whipped cream, for topping

Combine first 3 ingredients in a medium saucepan. Gradually stir in water. Cook over low heat, stirring constantly, until thick and clear. Stir small amount of hot mixture into egg yolks, then return yolks to hot mixture. Cook and stir one minute.

Remove from heat and add butter, zest, and juice. Return to heat for one minute, and stir until butter is melted and ingredients are well combined. Serve warm sauce over slices of gingerbread, topped with whipped cream.

ORANGE RUM CAKE

MY FIRST experience with rum was with this cake, my mother's recipe. My most recent was with a Bacardi and Coke, with a key lime squeezed over it. This is dedicated to my dear friend Silver Garza, a true connoisseur of this particular spirit.

Cake batter:
1 cup softened butter
2 cups sugar
2 eggs
2½ cups sifted flour
2 teaspoons baking powder
1 teaspoon baking soda
½ teaspoon salt
Zest of 2 large oranges and 1 lemon
1 cup buttermilk
1 cup pecans

Soaking syrup:
1 cup sugar
Juice of 2 large oranges
Juice of 1 lemon
2 tablespoons rum

Picking fruit at just the right time can make a world of difference when using fresh ingredients for baking. Peach pound cake during the summertime in Texas is heavenly, while citrus-based cakes like gingerbread with lemon sauce or orange rum cake are magical in the winter.

Preheat oven to 350 degrees, and grease and flour a bundt pan. In bowl, cream butter and 1 cup sugar. Add eggs one at a time. In another bowl, sift together flour, baking powder, baking soda, and salt. Add zest to creamed mixture, then add flour mixture alternately with buttermilk. Add pecans. Bake for 1 hour.

Boil sugar and fruit juices together for 3 minutes. Add rum. When cake has been out of the oven for approximately 5 minutes, poke holes with a skewer or toothpick and liberally brush syrup on top of the cake before inverting it. Quickly remove from pan onto a serving platter, and baste with remaining syrup.

ORANGE RUM CAKE

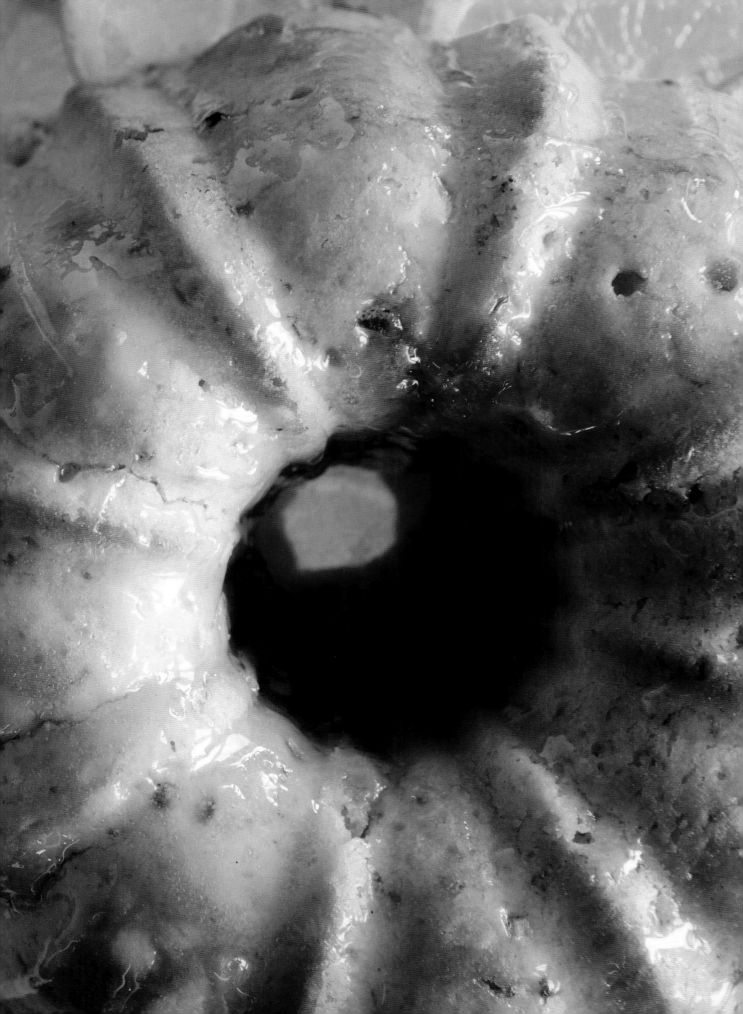

LEMON CHIFFON PIE

MY MOTHER's lemon chiffon cake was one of my absolute favorite desserts that she made. I loved how light and fluffy the cake was and the sweet and tart lemon flavor. I wasn't really into chocolate when I was growing up. I preferred pound cakes and this cake. Once I had a "pet" raccoon, or one that came around all the time. There was a little bowl I would use to leave water out for him. One time I shared a slice of my cake with him by putting it by his water bowl. It was the first time I realized that raccoons really do have to wash everything they eat. He picked up that slice of cake, stuck it in his water bowl, and was so annoyed when his paws came out clean.

In our family, Christmas and the Camp McCulloch Reunion were more celebrated than our birthdays. But one time I remember my mom made the lemon chiffon cake for my birthday. Once she finished, she thought it was too refined to serve for a 10-year-old's birthday, so she stuck it in the freezer to serve some other time. I actually found that damn cake when I was cleaning our her freezer almost 30 years later. Unfortunately, the recipe for her cake has been lost over the years, but a close second for my favorite desserts from my mother was her lemon meringue pie, a recipe I was able to find from her files.

For this recipe we added a little sugar to Hisako's recipe for merengue. It's not completely necessary, but it definitely adds a nice contrast to the tart lemon custard beneath.

Meringue topping:
3 egg whites
¼ teaspoon cream of tartar
½ cup superfine/caster sugar
1 teaspoon vanilla

Filling ingredients:
1¼ cups sugar
⅓ cup cornstarch
Dash salt
Zest of 2 lemons
2 tablespoons butter
⅓ cup lemon juice
1½ cups hot water
3 egg yolks, beaten
1 store-bought 9-inch pie crust, baked according to instructions and cooled

For meringue, place egg whites and cream of tartar in bowl of a stand mixer fitted with the whisk attachment. Beat until soft peaks form, then gradually add vanilla and sugar and continue beating until stiff peaks form, approximately 1 to 2 minutes.

For filling, combine first 6 ingredients. Add half of the hot water and stir vigorously. Add remaining water and combine well. Slowly add egg yolks. Cook over medium heat until mixture bubbles. Be careful not to burn. Pour mixture into pie shell, and top with meringue while filling is still hot. Make sure meringue completely covers filling right up to edge of crust. Bake 10 to 12 minutes or until meringue is golden. Remove from oven and cool on wire rack. Make sure pie is cooled completely before slicing.

A view from behind a window in my mother's house. We were always outside so much, it's not a view I often stopped to enjoy.

CHAPTER FOUR

LIFE ON THE RANCH

★ ★ ★

G ROWING UP on 500 acres of land is different than what most kids experience, especially kids from the city. When my brother, Butch, and I weren't in school, we were helping our family work the ranch, spending time at Roxie's, or spending time in our great big backyard. The memories I hold close include things like lying on Roxie's cool concrete porch to cool off from the summer heat; scampering down to Onion Creek on warm days to cool off; walking through fields of thick native grass, golden and shimmering in the sun, high as a horse's belly; hunting the land with my father and brother during dove season; and working. It seemed we were always working. But the work wasn't bad. It always kept me outside in a beautiful place.

I have a lot of fond memories of the ranch, but the thing I remember most is that it was hot. And dry. We first moved there in 1956, and that was during the drought of record for Texas. Onion Creek was completely dry. Trees were dying, and everything was hot and dusty. And then one day, it began to rain. A storm system had kicked up from a hurricane in the Gulf of Mexico, and it was fierce. I had never seen so much water in my life. I thought it was the Great Flood from the story of Noah's Ark, and I was terrified. For days there was water everywhere. The bridge over Onion Creek had a river of water running over it that was so fast that whole trees were being washed down and flipping over when they hit the bridge. After the storm finally passed, everything turned from bleak, dry, and dusty to verdant, with green grass and trees. But it was still hot. And it didn't help that we had no air-conditioning.

At night, you could see millions of stars. I would go to my grandparents' house, stand in the yard, and look up at the Milky Way. I could even see the different colors—silver, blue, red, and orange. Imagine the wonder I felt as a kid to see a blazing comet shoot across the dark night sky, with that exquisite stellar backdrop. My grandmother's house in Driftwood was purely magical. At that time, Austin was only itself a speck of light in the distance. Now the city light has encroached on our big black skies. You can see only a fraction of the stars you saw when I was a kid, and you certainly don't see the Milky Way anymore.

It was also lonely out on the ranch. There was nobody else around, except for my parents and grandparents. For school, we had to catch the bus early in the morning and ride for more than an hour to pick up other kids before getting there. At the end of the day, we wouldn't get home until 4:30 or 5 p.m. I would lie down in the big seat and take a nap on the way home. Eventually I knew exactly where the bus was driving, based on the sounds it made and the turns we took.

Back then, FM 1826 was just a narrow little road. Sometimes, when I went to stay at my grandparents house, I would make a game of counting the cars that drove by on the weekend. It wasn't a very fun game, because there really weren't many to count. Two on a Saturday was a big deal. A lot of times, Butch and I would just go around the property and shoot things. We both had little .22 rifles. We shot snakes, jackrabbits, birds, and old cans for target practice. And, of course, there were always chores to get through. We fed cows, fixed broken pens, built fences. One year, my parents gave me a prickly pear burner, which was basically a metal gas can with a spray pump. You lit the end, and using it like a small blowtorch, you could burn the needles off cactus so the cows could eat it. I was 10 years old. I don't imagine many parents nowadays would give a 10-year-old a combustible can with three gallons of gasoline to carry on his back. But those were different times.

Despite the chores and general horsing around, time passed slowly on the ranch. I swear the days were a week long. Nights were neverending, and it would take years for Christmas to come.

Camp Ben McCulloch–In Honor of Benjamin McCulloch

Camp Ben McCulloch was established just across from our property in 1896 as a reunion site for the United Confederate Veterans (UCV). It is the last such site still owned by the UCV's descendant group, the Sons and Daughters of the Confederacy. My grandfather, Bill Roberts, was the custodian for the camp for more than 50 years. Each year, the camp held a Reunion in honor of the Confederate veterans. Families would gather from miles around, to cook out, camp, and reconnect as family and friends. Today the camp is used as a public recreation facility managed by Hays County, often for family reunions, picnics, and music festivals.

Many people in Central Texas may know of Camp Ben McCulloch and even a little about the man for which it is named, but few probably realize the significance Benjamin McCulloch had on the history of Texas, and the entire South, for that matter.

Though originally from Tennessee, McCulloch moved to Texas in 1835 with one of his closest friends and neighbors, David Crockett. (Ben was joined by his brother, Henry McCulloch.)

They planned to meet Crockett's Tennessee Boys at Nacogdoches on Christmas Day, but Ben was bedridden with measles for several weeks. The brothers arrived too late at Nacogdoches but went on to San Antonio. By then, the Alamo had already fallen, along with their friend Crockett.

McCulloch joined the Texas army under Sam Houston in its retreat to East Texas and served in the famed Battle of San Jacinto, earning a commission of first lieutenant. Though McCulloch soon left the commission to return to Tennessee, he came back to Texas and in 1838 became a land surveyor. He soon joined the Texas Rangers as a lieutenant to Captain John Coffee "Jack" Hays and earned a reputation as an Indian fighter.

In 1839 he was elected to the Republic of Texas House of Representatives but returned to surveying and intermittent military service, including scouting during the Battle of Plum Creek against the Comanche. He then served as a scout for Captain Hays' Rangers. He and his brother, Henry, subsequently took part in the failed Somervell expedition and both escaped shortly before most of the Texans were captured, in December 1842.

In 1845 McCulloch was elected to the first Texas Legislature, following the state's entry into the Union. In the spring of 1846, he was appointed major general in command of all Texas militia west of the Colorado River, and he raised a company of Rangers that became Company A of Col. Hays' First Regiment of Texas Mounted Volunteers, known for their ability to regularly travel 250 miles in 10 days or less.

Texas seceded from the Union on February 1, 1861, and on February 14, McCulloch received a colonel's commission from Confederate President Jefferson Davis, which led to the appointment of brigadier general following the defeat of U.S. Army General Twigg's federal installations around San Antonio.

McCulloch was placed in command of the Indian Territory and set up headquarters at Little Rock. With the assistance of Brigadier General Albert Pike, he built alliances for the Confederacy with the Cherokee, Choctaw, and Creek nations.

McCulloch commanded the Confederate right wing at the Battle of Pea Ridge, where he was shot dead while scouting enemy positions. McCulloch's body was buried on the field at Pea Ridge but was later interred in the Texas State Cemetery in Austin.

The camp has long been known as the Reunion Grounds. Families of the Confederate Veterans came to the camp and stayed for two weeks each year. If you go there today, you can still see where little wooden signs are posted on trees with family names, designating reserved camping spots. My grandparents held the same spot for more than 50 years. The Reunion was held in July during a full moon so people could see better at night. There would be cookouts, baseball games, prayer meetings, and dancing to live music.

The dance floor was a large concrete slab framed by stone benches. Strands of white lights stretched above the space as a ceiling facade beneath the night sky. (In the waiting area at the Salt Lick, you'll see we recreated what I remember of the Camp Ben McCulloch dance floor.) I'll never forget staying up late, listening to music, and dancing under the stars while summer breezes swept through.

Every summer, I waited for the Reunion with great anticipation. More than 150 families showed up. For the big events on the weekends, we'd sometimes have around 1,000 people from all over the area. It was the only time throughout the year I was surrounded by other kids and it was the end of a quiet loneliness. We were a roving band of kids who would run around for two weeks, going from campsite to campsite to eat and play games. We'd go to Onion Creek to swim. And when we got older, we'd work at swiping beers from coolers in the beds of pickup trucks in the camp. The Reunion was also where I had my first date.

There was always a little carnival, with a Ferris wheel, cotton candy, popcorn, sodas, and a number of concessions selling hamburgers and hot dogs. It's actually where my father began selling his barbecue for the first time, long before the Salt Lick ever opened. In later years, he discontinued his stand because sales were decimating the other concessions. So he opened his own restaurant, and the rest is Driftwood history.

Camp Ben Mc-
Culloch is more
than just a place
for the annual
summer Reunion
each July. It's also
a place to remem-
ber those who gave
their lives for our
country. Without
them, there would
be no Texas.

MEMO
COL. WOODS
32ND TEXAS
LONE STAR
19

RIAL

REGIMENT

CAVALRY

CHAPTER   U.D.C

86

❧ LUPE AND CHRISTELLA ALVARADO ❧

W E   H A D a ranch hand named Guadalupe "Lupe" Ranchel Alvarado. He and his wife, Christella, lived in a little stone house on our property. When I wasn't in school, Lupe would pick up me and my brother around 7 in the morning to help him on the ranch. We built fences, chased cows, and did odd jobs. We would work for a couple of hours, and as the sun started to heat us up, Lupe would take us to his house for a snack. Their stone house had a rock porch with the best breeze. Lupe would drive up with my brother and me and tell Christella, "Feed these boys," so we could work.

She would pat out fresh flour tortillas and throw them on a griddle. Then she would take a large cast-iron skillet and start frying bacon. When the bacon was almost done, she would add potatoes and onions and let them cook for a while with the bacon before adding tomatoes, peppers, and eggs. She'd cook everything up together and serve us the entire skillet with the fresh tortillas for us to dip the eggs out with our hands. It was like eating a big communal bowl of migas without the cheese and crunched up tortilla chips. It was delicious.

Lupe would make salsa from little chile piquins and tomatoes he grew in the front garden. He'd mash them up together in a molcajete and hand it to us to try. I usually liked his salsa a lot. The piquins made the salsa so hot that he'd have to cut the heat using serrano peppers. In other words, Lupe liked his salsa hot. He had a habit of walking by his piquin bushes, picking a ripe chile, and popping it in his mouth like it was candy. I have no idea how he could handle the heat. To this day it's something I can't do. But Lupe loved his peppers.

Sometimes Lupe would drive us back by his house to see if Christella had anything good to eat for lunch before we'd go to Roxie's for our usual lunch break. When we were lucky, she'd have tacos, enchiladas, or grilled Mexican corn picked fresh off the ranch.

Lupe always diced up the fresh ingredients before mashing them into a fine sauce using a mortar and pestle.

LUPE'S CHILE PIQUIN SALSA

1 serrano
3 chile piquins
¼ white onion, chopped
½ ripe tomato, chopped
Salt and pepper to taste

Mash together in a Mexican molcajete.

MEXICAN GRILLED CORN WITH COTIJA

8 ears fresh corn, silks removed, husk on, soaked in cold water for 30 minutes
2 tablespoons canola oil
Salt and freshly ground black pepper
¼ cup mayonnaise
Juice of 2 limes
1 tablespoon cayenne pepper
¼ cup grated cotija cheese

Heat grill to high. Grill corn until charred on all sides, 10 minutes or so. Remove from grill and cut off kernels with sharp knife. Heat a skillet over medium high. Add corn and remaining ingredients and cook, stirring occasionally, until creamy and heated through.

AFTER A LONG DAY of working on the ranch, we would drink beer, or cerveza, as Lupe called it. The first thing you did when you left the ranch house for work was fill up the water cooler with ice and water. The second thing you did was fill up Lupe's beer cooler with ice and beer. Those weren't the Styrofoam chests you see today. They were metal and wood and heavy, and they had real latches that held the lid down. They were lined with zinc, and they kept the beer really cold. We stored the coolers in the bed of the pickup truck, against the cab on the driver's side.

As soon as work was over, Lupe and his workers put the equipment up, pulled beers from the ice chest, sat on the tailgate, and reminisced about the day's work, in that order.

One glorious weekend, our parents were in Austin, bidding on bridge jobs, and my grandparents were at the coast with some friends (one of the few times they ever went anywhere). Lupe's wife, Christella, had to attend a family function in Kyle with one of her sisters. So my brother and I had to spend the weekend with Lupe, and we drank a lot of cerveza.

Lupe was an aspiring guitarist. He had a small amplifier and one electric guitar. One night after sunset and a full day's work, he decided to teach us how to sing. He brought out his guitar and began to play. Like the lyrics say from that Janis Joplin song, we sang every song that Lupe knew. They were all in Spanish and I have no idea what half of them were about, but we had a good time singing at the top of our lungs out in the middle of the country. Every time our throats got dry from the singing, he let us have another beer.

Singing and drinking leads to a hearty appetite. Around midnight, we got extremely hungry. Lupe had a young goat, or cabrito, that he had been saving for a special dinner, but he decided we should have it that night. We built a fire, got a grill, and put a skillet on it. Lupe slaughtered and butchered the goat, seasoned it, and cooked it up over the open fire. We sat outside and ate the grilled meat on warm tortillas, with more cold cerveza, and stared at the stars.

The key to this is using fresh corn on the cob when it's in season. You can use frozen if you're in a pinch, but the flavor just isn't as golden sweet.

This is my father's 1959 Buick Electra 225. Everyone else had a black Lincoln, so he wanted this. It was the first car with electric windows that anyone around here had ever seen.

It was a hot night. We pulled mattresses off the beds from inside and put them on a flatbed truck. That night we—the Lords of the Land—slept well beneath a canopy of the brightest stars you could ever imagine.

TOWARD THE END of summer, my brother, my father, and I always looked forward to bird season. The autumn air was cool and crisp, and the sun would creep over the fields early in the morning when we began our hunts. We once had healthy populations of both quail and dove on our property. But the fire ants have pushed the quail out over the years. My brother, my father, and I could usually bet on getting a bunch of dove. We hunted through the sunflower fields to flush out birds or by the ponds at sunset. I remember the long golden rays of sunlight that would shower the blades of grass in the pasture. Just before sunset, the light would give a gold shimmer to the grass and just at the right moment, the seed heads would light up with a sun-kissed glow and seemed to explode like a light bulb turning on.

When my dad went with us, he used an old single-shot 12-gauge that belonged to my great-grandfather from the Civil War. Whatever birds we brought home, my mom used for dinner that night. A lot of people will use only the breast of the dove or quail, but she used the whole thing. She would sometimes fry them, and I loved to eat the crunchy little bones. I didn't know then that eating the whole bird was common in other parts of the world, like Europe and Asia. It's not for everybody, but it's a delicacy I still enjoy.

Roxie and Hisako always fried quail or dove, treating it like fried chicken or venison. The only difference is that they didn't use a wet component. They used only dry seasoned flour before frying the birds. Roxie would serve it with mashed potatoes while Hisako would serve it with white rice, and she'd add a little garlic to flavor the frying oil. At the Salt Lick, our way of serving quail includes stuffing it with sausage rice and roasting it. We serve it with a Texas Ruby Red grapefruit glaze and a jicama-grapefruit salsa. This recipe is my take on how beautiful quail can be when served with some of Texas' great local produce.

SALT LICK ROASTED QUAIL WITH
GRAPEFRUIT GLAZE AND JICAMA-GRAPEFRUIT SALSA

4 whole quail, rinsed and dried
Salt and pepper to taste

Brine:
¼ cup kosher salt
4 cups water
4 bay leaves

Stuffing:
1 cup wild rice
2 ½ cups chicken broth
2 carrots, finely chopped
2 celery stalks, finely chopped
1 onion, finely chopped
2 shallots, minced
2 cloves garlic, minced
½ cup chopped apricots
½ cup toasted chopped pecans

Glaze:
4 tablespoons orange blossom honey
Juice of 1 to 2 Texas Ruby Red grapefruits
Salt and pepper to taste

Jicama-grapefruit salsa:
1 grapefruit, cut into bite-size segments
1 cup jicama slices (thin bite-size strips)
2 cloves garlic, chopped
¼ cup chopped red onion
2 teaspoons chopped chives
½ red bell pepper, cut into thin bite-size strips
1 serrano, seeded and minced
2 tablespoons lime juice
2 tablespoons orange blossom honey

You can play around with the different salsas you use for this quail dish. Typically, it's best with something that has a little citrus in it. The best time to make this with the grapefruit salsa is in the wintertime, when Texas grapefruit are in the peak of season.

For the brine: Combine ingredients in saucepan and bring to a boil. Let cool to room temperature, and submerge quail in liquid. Brine 2 to 6 hours but no longer, as the meat will become too salty. Remove from brine, pat dry, and set aside for cooking.

For stuffing: In a covered saucepan, boil the first 7 ingredients for 20 to 25 minutes, or until rice is tender. Cool, add apricots and pecans, and toss well. Reserve.

For glaze: Combine ingredients in a saucepan over medium low heat. Whisk constantly until honey incorporates grapefruit juice. Season to taste, and reserve.

For jicama-grapefruit salsa: Toss all ingredients until well mixed. Refrigerate.

For cooking the quail: Preheat oven to 450 degrees. Stuff each quail with ¼ to ½ cup stuffing, depending on size. Season to taste. *NOTE: Because quail has been brined, go light on the salt.*

Place quail on wire rack, leaving space between each. Roast 10 to 12 minutes. (Shorter roasting will give you quail that are juicy, succulent, and a little pink on the inside.) Remove from oven and baste with grapefruit glaze. Return to oven and cook for an additional 2 to 3 minutes. Remove from oven and baste one more time. Let rest under loose tent of foil for 5 to 10 minutes. Serve immediately, garnished with jicama-grapefruit salsa.

GREEN ONION AND CHEESE SOUFFLÉ

When I was growing up, we cultivated a lot of different vegetables to sell to grocery stores in Austin. We had one whole field of green onions. Although I love the taste of green onions today, I hated green onions when I was little. To harvest them, we had to scour that whole field. Because it involved so much bending down, we crawled along the ground to get them. By the time we were finished, we were sticky with onion juice and covered in gooey dirt. We'd start sweating during the heat of the day, and when we wiped our faces, the dirt and onion juice would get all over and it would stir up an army of gnats. It was awful. It would take days of bathing to get rid of that onion scent.

2 tablespoons unsalted butter

3 tablespoons flour

1 cup milk, room temperature

½ cup grated Gruyère cheese

½ cup grated Parmigiano-Reggiano cheese

½ cup chopped pancetta, optional

1 to 2 bunches green onions, cleaned and sliced on the bias into ½-inch pieces

1 tablespoon butter

2 teaspoons Dijon mustard

4 egg yolks

Salt and pepper to taste

8 egg whites

1 teaspoon cream of tartar

Preheat the oven to 375 degrees, and butter a 1½-quart soufflé mold. Preheat a medium saucepan over medium high heat. Add butter and melt until frothy. Add flour, reduce heat to medium, and cook, stirring constantly for 2 to 3 minutes, creating a roux. Remove pan from heat, and add the milk, whisking vigorously. Return pot to the heat, and bring the mixture to a boil to thicken (This is a basic white sauce). Again, remove pan from heat, and add cheeses, stirring well to melt.

In large skillet, cook pancetta (if using) over medium heat. When fully cooked and a little crispy, add green onions and sauté briefly. If you are not including the pancetta, simply sauté green onions in 1 tablespoon butter.

Add green onions, mustard, and yolks to cheese sauce. Taste and season with salt and pepper. Season well or over-season slightly, because this mixture will be diluted by the egg whites later. Let mixture cool completely.

Whisk egg whites in copper bowl to a soft peak. In three stages, carefully fold egg whites into soufflé base. Transfer mixture to soufflé mold. Bake for 30 minutes, or until risen and lightly browned on top. The soufflé should jiggle only slightly when finished.

Onion Creek–The Nile of Driftwood

I grew up on Onion Creek. For me, it's more than just a windy little river whose headwaters start northeast of Blanco near Henly and flow southwest through the Hill Country into the Colorado River. When I was younger and came home from school in the afternoon, I didn't have friends nearby to play with. Instead, I explored on our property and would always find myself along the banks of Onion Creek, where sprawling cypress and pecan trees loomed overhead, hillsides of Turk's cap flowered in bright red blooms, and wild watercress grew along the gravel banks. The creek cut deep into much of our land, leaving gently sloping ravines for me to wander. Some of the ravine walls were covered in ferns from natural springs that seeped from the rock into the creek.

As a family, we spent Saturday afternoons by the creek, fishing for perch and catfish and swimming in its cool waters with the fish, turtles, and, sometimes, snakes. My mother would fry up catfish and hush puppies and serve them with a spring slaw of vegetables from her garden.

The creek was once referred to as the Garrapatas (Spanish for sheep tick) as early as 1720 but was predominantly called Onion Creek by 1830. (For potential ranchland purchasers, it wasn't appealing to buy land that included the word "tick" in the name.) The creek got its present name, it is said, from the early settlers of Stephen F. Austin's Little Colony who lived near the mouth of the stream, where it flows into the Colorado River, and found wild onions growing in abundance along its banks.

The cypress trees along the banks of Onion Creek played an important role in the early history of Driftwood, bringing shingle makers to the area to use the trees for shingle production. In 1839 Texas President Mirabeau B. Lamar appointed a number of men called the Capital Commission to choose a site for a permanent capital of the new Republic of Texas. When they chose a site on the Colorado River near a little town called Waterloo, they presented as one of their reasons that about 18 miles southwest, on Onion Creek and the Blanco River, grew a magnificent stand of cypress trees from which much lumber could be made.

Eventually the capital site at Waterloo was renamed Austin. The stand of cypress mentioned by the Capital Commission began the present Driftwood area. Though much of the trees were left alone, many stumps along the creek are evidence that some were cut to make and sell shingles in the late 1800s.

For our family, as with many families that grew up in that area, Onion Creek was a source of life, a veritable Nile River for our region. As it has meandered through those hills, with floodwaters and droughts depositing and exposing various rich soils, it has not only delivered water but cultivated excellent farming soil, lush vegetation, and even driftwood for firewood and building—which is how Driftwood got its name. For some, Onion Creek is just a creek. For me, it's the Nile of Driftwood.

The cool waters of Onion Creek were like an oasis for me and my family. Whenever we wanted a break from the hustle and bustle of daily life, we'd come here to escape and enjoy the beauty of nature.

CATFISH WITH HUSH PUPPIES

BEFORE MY DAD quit the bridge business, spending time as a family was sometimes difficult. But once or twice a year, we would make up for it by spending a whole day down on the banks of Onion Creek. It was the only time that all four of us—my mother, my father, my brother, and I—would spend an entire day as a family. There were no phones, no visitors, no last-minute tasks on the ranch, no distractions at all. It was just cane poles, a creek, afternoon swimming, and a big catfish fry.

We first moved to Driftwood in the middle of a drought. Everything was dry, dusty, and brown. But once a few big storms came through, the whole property was lush with life and it was most exquisite on Onion Creek. There were bends with gentle rapids that opened into deep pools with clear blue water. The trees were flush with brilliant foliage that whispered in the breezes blowing through the valley. In the summer, you could hear cicadas buzzing and frogs croaking, especially at dusk. Onion Creek was an oasis for us that served as a rejuvenating refuge for our little family escapes.

On the morning of the big day, we'd pack up our truck as if we were going camping, with picnic blankets and chairs, cookout equipment, fishing gear, and some fresh clothes. We'd drive to the trailhead above the creek and unload everything by sunup, carrying it all down a small hillside to a sandy point on the water. My dad would have a spade and a coffee can and take my brother and me to dig up worms while my mother set up everything. We'd gather our bait and set off fishing all morning. My mother would have a midday snack ready for us and then worked on preparing for our fish later.

Inevitably, one of us would break the seal and end up falling in the water before the rest of us would join for a refreshing swim. In the springtime, the water was still cool, but not too cold to get in. But the summertime was always so hot that we could hardly wait to submerge ourselves in the crisp, clean water. I remember I would relax on the shore, looking up at the pecan, oak, and mulberry trees that shaded us. Along the hillside was a cliff alive with spiraling ferns that grew from the spring water seeping from the hillside. In history class I learned of a legend that the Aztecs came up toward Texas to hide their gold. One particular little cave beneath the ferns was, I always imagined, a secret spot where the Aztecs must have hidden their treasure.

My brother and I would skip stones in the creek and swim in the afternoon while my parents prepared our catfish feast. My mom cooked up all of the fish and made her version of hush puppies. (Roxie made the more traditional kind, but Hisako added mushroom, onion, creamed corn, and jicama to give them a little extra flavor and texture.) Those few times a year that we would escape for a day on Onion Creek were some of the best memories I have with my family. It was the only time we all did something together, the only time I ever saw my parents relax, and the only time I can remember relishing the natural beauty of a creek that ran through our own backyard.

There are some meals that taste right only when they're enjoyed in a particular place. For me, fried catfish with hush puppies should always belong on a picnic blanket along the banks of Onion Creek.

Fried catfish:
3 cups yellow cornmeal
3 cups white flour
1 tablespoon salt
1 tablespoon granulated garlic
1 tablespoon cayenne pepper

Mix all ingredients together. *NOTE: Sample and add more salt if necessary.*

10-quart Dutch oven, filled ¾ full with lard and 2 tablespoons bacon grease
4 10-ounce boneless fresh catfish fillets, cut in half

Heat lard and bacon grease to 375 degrees. Wash fillets and coat with cornbread mixture. Add four fillets at a time to oil and cook approximately 18 minutes. When fillets float, bubbles subside, and pointed edge of fillet begins to curl, remove and allow to drain on paper towels. Serve hot.

Hush puppies:
2 cups cornmeal
2 cups flour
1 tablespoon salt
2 tablespoons baking powder
½ teaspoon granulated garlic
½ teaspoon cayenne pepper
1 tablespoon sugar
2 eggs, beaten
1 cup cream corn
1 cup whole kernel corn, drained
2 medium white onions, finely minced
1 cup milk

Heat a 10-quart Dutch oven filled ¾ full with lard and 2 tablespoons bacon grease to 350 degrees. (Or if you have just finished making fried catfish, use the same heated ingredients and bring the temperature down to 350 degrees.) Combine all dry ingredients well, add eggs and mix. Then add corn and onions, and mix. Mix in milk, and let stand five minutes until it begins to rise. Drop rounded tablespoons into hot oil, and cook for 3½ minutes. When hush puppies float to top, turn once and let fry. Keep turning until they are an even golden brown.

CATFISH, HUSH PUPPIES,
AND JALAPEÑO CORNBREAD

JALEPEÑO CORNBREAD

THIS ISN'T in the recipe, but sometimes when Hisako was making this cornbread for us at home, she would render the lard out of bacon and use the leftover cracklins in the cornbread batter. It's a little extra work, but it's worth it.

¼ cup melted butter
¼ cup minced onions
½ pounds sausage, finely chopped
3 fresh jalapeños, seeded and finely chopped
2 cups yellow cornmeal
½ cup flour
1 teaspoon salt
2 teaspoons baking powder
1 teaspoon baking soda
2 cups buttermilk
2 eggs
1 8-ounce can cream corn
2 tablespoons bacon grease

In skillet melt butter over low heat. Add onions and cook till translucent. Add sausage and jalapeños, and cook 1 more minute. Remove from heat, keep warm, reserve. Preheat oven to 350 degrees. Mix 5 dry ingredients well. Whip buttermilk and eggs together. Add buttermilk mixture to dry ingredients, and mix well. Fold in sausage mixture and pan scrapings. Fold in creamed corn. Let rest while heating skillet and grease. Place bacon grease in 9-inch cast-iron skillet, and heat in oven. When grease begins to smoke, remove skillet. Stir cornbread mixture, carefully pour into hot grease, return to oven, and bake for 30 minutes or until top is brown and a toothpick inserted into middle of pan comes out clean.

✤ THURMAN'S HUNTING BREAKFASTS ✤

EACH YEAR for deer season, my dad would host a big breakfast for friends and family. They all showed up before sunrise, and my dad would have a whole feast prepared, with a big skillet of scrambled eggs, bacon, refried beans, tortillas, pork ribs, and a big pot of coffee. He cooked on a commercial flat grill at the restaurant and served everything family style.

After breakfast, they would all go off to different spots around Driftwood to hunt. They usually trickled back by midmorning for coffee and leftovers and to compare their trophy bucks and hunting accounts for the early part of the day.

Al Godwin, a friend of my dad's from Dallas, would always come down to stay over the night before. He and my dad would sit up and drink beer and eat hard-boiled eggs. It was the only time of year that my dad would drink beer. He would drink only two, and it was always Löwenbräu. They sat around the table and told old war stories while they shelled their eggs and ate them. One time Butch and I planted a few raw eggs in their bowl and watched from the other room as they smashed into them. They got so mad, and my brother and I ran into the other room, snickering and laughing. We paid for it the next morning, though. We would be up ready to get going and Al would be struggling to put his knee brace on. It always took forever, but we eventually got the big hunting day started.

BRISKET AND EGG TACO

2 ounces butter
½ cup diced yellow onion
2 fresh whole serrano peppers, thinly sliced
1 cup diced cooked potatoes (or 1 cup Salt Lick potato salad for best flavor)
1 cup diced Roma tomatoes
1 pound chopped smoked brisket, warm
16 eggs, beaten
Salt and pepper to taste
10 to 12 tortillas

Heat a skillet with butter. Add onion and serrano, and sauté until onion is translucent. Add potato and tomato, and sauté until warm. Add the chopped beef. Pour in eggs, and cook until they begin to slightly firm. Season to taste. Place egg mixture on a tortilla and serve. Serves 6 to 8.

REFRIED BEANS

IF THE KEY to great sausage is pork, the key to great refried beans is lard. You can substitute with vegetable oil or bacon grease, but there really is nothing that adds better flavor than lard.

¼ cup lard (vegetable oil will work)
3 cups pinto beans, cooked and drained
½ teaspoon salt
¼ teaspoon coarse ground black pepper
½ cup chicken stock

Heat lard over medium high in a large deep skillet or pot. Add beans and use a potato masher to combine the beans into the lard. Add salt and pepper to taste, and incorporate. Add chicken stock (add more or less, depending on how thick you want the beans). Let beans set up and cook a bit. Transfer to a large griddle on medium high heat. Using a spatula, turn the beans over and over, letting them become crispy and caramelized between folding. You want a thick, smooth consistency. Serves 6 to 8. *NOTE: You can use canned pinto beans, but if you have the time, it's best to cook raw beans in slow cooker overnight.*

Driftwood got its name for all of the wood that would be deposited along the banks of Onion Creek after big floods. What people rarely realize is the amazing soil that also drifted down those waters that has gifted this area with wonderful farming land.

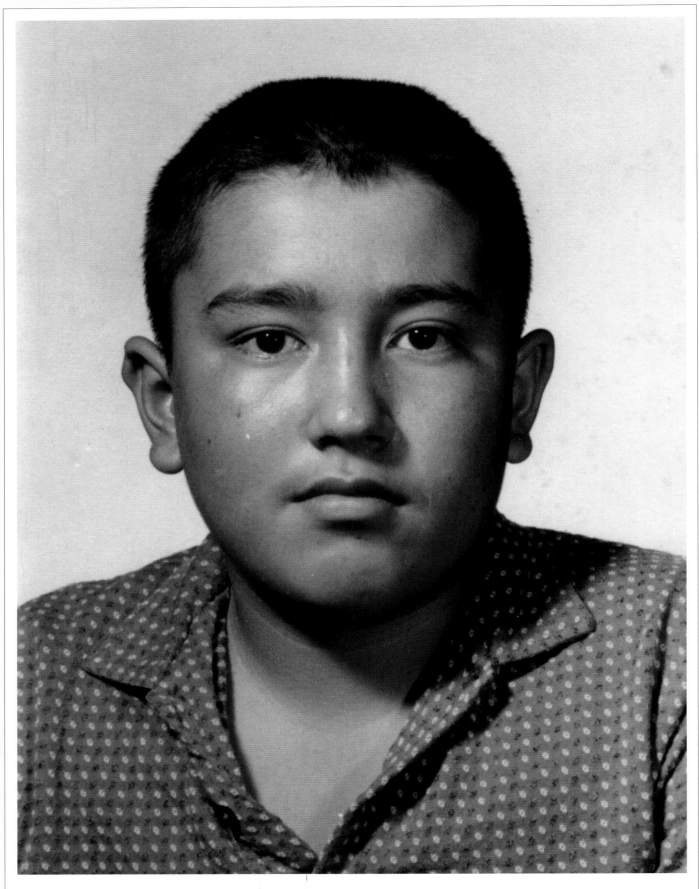

Thurman "Butch" Lee Roberts, Jr.
16 March 1949 – 17 September 1968

★ ★ ★

My Brother, "Butch"

★ ★ ★

I HAD A BROTHER who was only a couple of years older than I. His name was Thurman Lee Roberts, Jr., after my dad, but we called him Butch. He and I grew up doing just about everything together. Whether it was a weekend at Roxie's, hunting dove in the fields, or making mischief while working on the ranch with Lupe, we were always together. After he graduated from high school, he went to UT and got a job through a family friend, Ed Hammel, working construction on apartment complexes in Austin.

One day I had stayed home sick from school. It was a stormy day in September, with thunder and lightning all around. My parents had left to drop off an order of spices to a customer, when the phone rang. It was a nurse from Brackenridge Hospital in Austin. She said something had happened to my brother. That was long before cell phones, and my parents couldn't be reached. So I drove to the hospital alone. When I got there, Ed was in the waiting area. I noticed he had been crying. He looked at me and said he was "so sorry." And then he left. My brother was dead.

Butch had been working on a construction site and had slipped from the second floor. He hit his head on the way down. I sat alone in the waiting room for a little while, waiting for my parents. The highway patrol had pulled them over and told them to come to Austin regarding one of their sons. I had walked outside for some air right when they were pulling up to the hospital. It was still raining really hard. I climbed into their truck and told them what had happened. My father didn't say a word. He just sat there. But my mother started crying so hard that she fell to the floorboard. Later, my grandparents showed up and Roxie became hysterical. She kept crying, "What are we going to do without Butch?"

A few days later, they had a large funeral and tons of people came. I didn't go. I just couldn't be there. I stayed back home, and a former girlfriend, Patti, came over to keep me company. Everything sort of went silent and still at that point in my life. Sunday dinners at Roxie's stopped. My father's big hunting breakfasts ended. It was as if the entire family splintered in a million pieces. I had another year of high school before I left for college, and around that same time my parents started the Salt Lick. They poured all their energy into the restaurant, almost as a way to manage their grief from losing Butch. As they say, it takes a lot of blood, sweat, and tears to build something great, and building the Salt Lick took a lot of all three.

The situation was hard for everybody. No parent should have to outlive their child. I was fortunate to have a second family open its home to me. Raymond and Betty Jo Whisenant were part of a family that had been in the Driftwood and Dripping Springs area for a long time. The portion of our property where we have planted most of our vineyards is part of the original Whisenant Homestead from the early 1800s. Their son Ray was, and still is, a brother of mine.

Mrs. Whisenant was always concerned that I wasn't taking good care of myself after Butch passed away. She told me she would always have the door to their home open for me. Not only did she follow through on that promise but she also made sure to chicken fry a few slices of Spam for me and leave fixings so that I could make a sandwich. Since I had free range of her cupboard, I would make a few additions to the average fried spam between two pieces of bread.

If it weren't for the Whisenants' kindness, I would have had no point of reference. Spam sandwiches aren't the most gourmet meal, but they will always have a place in my memory. They represent a warm generosity from a family when I needed a family connection most of all. This is a simple recipe, but it's layered with a whole lot of heart.

SCOTT'S SPAM SANDWICHES

2 tablespoons vegetable oil

4 slices Spam from a can

1 cup flour

Garlic salt and pepper to taste

2 slices toast

Peanut butter and grape jelly

3 slices American cheese

Mayonnaise and mustard to taste

A few slices white onion

A few slices tomato

A few slices green bell pepper

Sweet pickle, sliced

Iceberg lettuce leaves

Heat oil on medium in frying pan. Dredge the Spam in flour seasoned with garlic salt and pepper. Sauté Spam to brown on both sides. Remove from heat, season, and set aside. Dress one slice of toast with peanut butter and jelly. *NOTE: My mature palate would probably use peach or fig preserves today.* Add a slice of American cheese. Add two slices of Spam side-by-side on top of the American cheese. On a second slice of toast, spread mayonnaise and, if you like, mustard. Add one slice of American cheese and two more slices of Spam side-by-side. Add vegetables. Sandwich pieces of toast together. Serves 1.

The two parallel rock lines in this picture are the borders of where Roxie's garden used to be. She was out there at all times of the year, tending the myriad vegetables she would plant.

❧ DRIFTWOOD ROMANCE ❧

WHEN I WAS younger, I met a girl from a nearby ranch named Debbie Tracy who bowled me over. The first time I saw her, we were at a Friday night high school football game. That cute little blond girl walked by with one of her friends, and it felt like there were thunderbolts all around. I was sitting on the hood of my red Chevy Impala, and she grabbed my foot and pulled me off the hood. She was one of the prettiest girls I'd ever seen. She had just moved to the area two weeks earlier. Her parents had bought the grocery store in Dripping Springs. We became inseparable for two years.

Debbie was my first young love. We would sit up and talk on the phone for hours, go to all the football games together, and ride my motorcycle all over the place. I had a little Honda that I rode on the back roads and pastures around home. During the summer I took her on rides through ditches and bumps in the pastures, and she would laugh hysterically (except for the few times she incurred muffler burns on her legs).

Her dad was really nice and would sometimes invite me over for dinner. He cooked up delicious steaks on a little backyard grill. Debbie's mother made great big salads with Green Goddess dressing. It was the first time I'd ever had dressing like that, and I'll never forget how amazing it tasted, especially with a steak dinner. I liked it so much, I would even put it on scrambled eggs at breakfast.

GREEN GODDESS DRESSING

½ clove of garlic
¼ teaspoon sea salt
¼ teaspoon dry mustard
⅛ teaspoon cayenne pepper
¼ teaspoon anchovy paste
2 teaspoons lemon juice
1 cup mayonnaise
½ cup heavy cream
¼ cup finely chopped parsley
1 teaspoon chopped chives

Crush garlic. Add salt, mustard, cayenne, and anchovy paste. Stir in remaining ingredients, cover, and refrigerate. *NOTE: Some recipes also include tarragon. If you want to try that taste, add 1 tablespoon chopped fresh tarragon or 1 teaspoon dried crumbled tarragon.*

LOVER'S CHICKEN BREAST

AFTER HIGH SCHOOL, I lived at home for a while before going to college at the University of Texas. A girl who worked at the Salt Lick for my dad lived on a ranch right across the creek from Camp Ben McCulloch (The names are withheld to protect the guilty). It was an old ranchstead, with a great big family house and a small side house for servants' quarters. The girl's parents traveled a lot, and her grandparents lived in the big family house. She convinced them to let her live in the little side house.

Sometimes, late at night, I'd sneak over to the Camp Ben McCulloch property. At the creek, I would strip off my clothes and, holding them above my head to keep them dry, swim across. I'd put my clothes back on, hike up the bluff to the houses, and sneak into her little cottage.

One night, as I was quietly making my exit, the family house front porch light came on and the door slammed open. It was a full moon, and I could see a big man (her grandfather) swinging a huge 12-gauge shotgun in the air. He was wearing only an undershirt and boxer shorts, but he had managed to throw on his cowboy boots and a big cowboy hat. He looked like a Texas Ranger.

I lost my breath and hit the ground. I broke into a cold sweat and prayed he wouldn't see me. After he looked around, he went back in and shut the door. I hopped up and hit the tree line running, thinking I had it made. But then the family dog started barking. The door swung back open, and I heard the gun go off and the shot gun pellets hitting the leaves of the tree above me. I ran so fast I nearly fell over myself. I crossed the creek without keeping my clothes dry and hurried back to Roxie's house, where I was living at the time.

Once I calmed down, I swiped a bottle of Wild Turkey from the cabinet and headed out to a point on our property that overlooked her ranch. I sat on a chair and took a swig, thanking the sweet Lord I'd made it home. While reliving the event in my mind, I thought to myself, "That man sure looked like a Texas Ranger, but thank God he didn't shoot like one."

Hill Country Compound Butter:
1 serrano chile
1 teaspoon mashed shallot
2 cloves garlic
Olive oil
Salt
6 tablespoons butter
1 tablespoon lime juice
1 teaspoon black pepper
1 teaspoon finely chopped cilantro
1 teaspoon chile powder
1 teaspoon chopped fresh rosemary
1 teaspoon chives

4 chicken breasts, skin on
Salt and pepper to taste

Toast serrano and shallot in dry cast-iron skillet until blackened on all sides. Remove serrano peel and stem, cut in half lengthwise, remove seeds and white membranes, and finely chop. Mash roasted shallot. Preheat oven to 350 degrees.

It may be healthier to prepare this dish with skinless chicken breasts, but in the interest of this story of young love, we suggest you leave the skin on as it imparts the most flavor, which is what makes all of our stories of young love so special.

Place garlic on a piece of aluminum foil, drizzle with little olive oil and salt, fold aluminum foil over garlic, and crimp to make airtight pouch. Bake pouch for about 30 minutes, until garlic is soft and golden. Place butter in bowl of food processor along with remaining ingredients. Scrape in garlic, oil, and salt from pouch as well. Pulse food processor until all ingredients are chopped and combined. To develop flavors fully, let rest 1 hour.

Preheat oven to 400 degrees. Clean, wash, and pat dry chicken breasts. Gently raise skin on breast and insert ¾ of compound butter. Press down to spread. Keep skin on chicken. Place chicken on sheet pan on wire rack. Rub remaining butter on top of skin and season. Place in oven for 25 to 30 minutes, until golden and cooked through.

MRS. HASSONG'S POPOVERS

I WAS BORN in Kaufman in East Texas while my father was building bridges in the area. We lived there for a few years before we all moved to our property in Driftwood, in 1956. A woman named Mrs. Ruth Hassong used to look after us. She had a son they called Little John, who was physically disabled. She always had him set up in the living room, where he could watch TV and she could see him while she worked around the house. When we stayed over, she would make us all popovers. I was always amazed at how the dough seemed to explode over the top of the muffin tins.

One night we were staying over, and a big storm blew in. The rain was torrential and the wind was howling. I was only 3 or 4 years old, and I was terrified. Then there was this loud sound that seemed to come from everywhere. It sounded like a train. We soon realized that it was, in fact, a tornado—or a cyclone, as they call them in East Texas. We all clamored to a safe part of the house. I was crying, and my brother kept saying things to try to make me laugh. The storm finally passed, and the house remained unharmed. The next day, I went outside and the landscape was a mess. I walked over to the old smokehouse, and I'll never forget seeing hundreds of spears of hay sticking straight out of the wooden door like a bunch of porcupine quills.

It wasn't long before we moved to the Hill Country, where tornadoes are less common. I'll never forget the hay needles on the side of that smokehouse. And I'll never forget Mrs. Hassong's popovers. (Mrs. Hassong once told me that the key to a good popover is the pan. Once you find a good one, don't let it go.)

2 eggs
1 cup milk
1 cup flour
½ teaspoon salt

Heat oven to 425 degrees. Heavily grease 6 custard cups or 8 muffin cups. Beat eggs slightly. Add remaining ingredients. Stir with fork until smooth. Do not overbeat. Fill greased custard cups ½ full or muffin cups ¾ full. Bake 40 to 45 minutes, or until deep golden brown. Remove from cups immediately.

The Camp Ben McCulloch summer Reunions still go on to this day. Each year, families mark their camping spot for the next year with a little wooden sign bearing their name. It's a primitive reservation system, but it's something that's worked for more years than I've been alive.

The entrance to the Salt Lick. The rock bollards were constructed at the insistence of my wife, Susan. I left town one weekend for a fishing trip, and when I returned they were there.

CHAPTER FIVE

SALT LICK BARBECUE

★ ★ ★

WELL, I GUESS you want to hear about the barbecue. It took about 100 years before the recipes we serve at the Salt Lick today were even ready to share with the general public. Years of family history, hardship, and ingenuity are reduced to a handful of barbecue dishes that represent my family's story. Our recipes are basically their recipes, based on technique and freshness.

My father had no idea what he was creating when he dug his boot heel into the ground, drew a circle in the dirt around him with a barbecue fork, and outlined a barbecue pit. Sure, he wanted to serve foods that reminded him of home, and barbecue was the best way to do that. But he anticipated only a small weekend operation that served his community. He never would have imagined people trekking across the county, the state, or even the country to eat what he was cooking over an open pit. But sometimes it's the simple things that attract the most attention.

For the first time, we're opening our recipe book to you. It's because of loyal customers that the Salt Lick has given a name and identity to my family's history. Some things we are happy to share generously with you. With other things, like our secret sauce, you'll just have to head back to Driftwood for more.

*The only way
to truly enjoy
great barbecue is
when it's shared
family style.*

SALT LICK BAR-B-QUE SAUCE

THE SALT LICK BAR-B-QUE SAUCE is the one ingredient we use from start to finish with our food. We use it before we start to cook meats, we use it to baste while we're cooking, and we serve it at every table as the perfect condiment for your meal. We even included it in a few of our side dishes as well. Long before we started to bottle and sell it, people would stop by the restaurant and request a to-go sampler of it. Now we sell it at the restaurant, in stores, and online. I've had people tell me that when they can't get Salt Lick barbecue, they'll at least use their home stash of our sauce to doctor up barbecue from somewhere else.

We use a vinegar-sugar sauce rather than a tomato-based sauce, which would burn and add an acrid taste to the barbecue. Ours is essentially a Southeastern style of sauce that has been Texa-fied with a list of ingredients—cayenne and chili powder, to name a few. When the roots of this sauce left the Carolinas with my relatives in the 1870s, I am sure it had no cayenne pepper in it. But over the years it has taken on more of the terroir from which it is served. I can tell you that there are more than 32 ingredients. But if you knew each individual one, I'd simply have to kill you.

You'll notice that the list for this recipe includes only one ingredient. The truth is, I just can't tell you what's in it. We can't give away all of our secrets. But I can tell you where it came from and that it has its roots in a family's story that spans more than a 120 years in Driftwood.

1 bottle Salt Lick Bar-B-Que Sauce (Original Recipe, Chipotle, or Spicy Recipe)

SALT LICK DRY RUB

THE SALT LICK DRY RUB is a simple recipe with three ingredients. The trick is figuring out the right grind size. We have had to adjust this in order to sell it commercially in bottles. Feel free to adjust as you see fit.

7.5 ounces Morton salt
3 ounces black pepper, medium grind
1½ ounces cayenne pepper, ground

Combine well before use.

700

BY THE NUMBERS
During the week, the Salt Lick serves an average of 700 people a day.

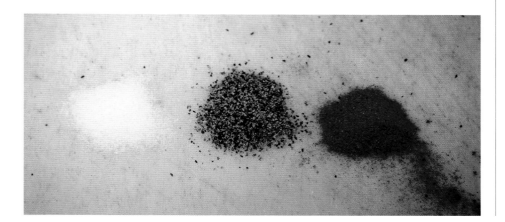

Wood: Solid as an Oak

Despite the nice marketing ring that the term "mesquite-grilled" brings to the table, barbecuing with mesquite wood was more for necessity than for flavor for most Mexican vaqueros working cattle in South and West Texas. But before cattle ranching moved through this part of Texas, much of the land was grassland, not the cactus-and-mesquite desert land we might pass through today. The great transition of the land began when the buffalo and Comanche were driven off and cattle began overgrazing the prairieland, giving way to thorny mesquite that now dominates the landscape. New settlements also prevented the natural brush fires that would help keep the grasses flourishing. Typically, mesquite burns very hot, with a richly flavored smoke. That is, only if the wood has been aged 18 to 24 months. When it's green, it still has all of its oils and imparts a bitter taste. Aging allows for a richer flavor that is almost a spice unto itself.

Throughout Texas, the early settlers used whatever they could find to start fires and cook meat. But perhaps the Central Texans were most fortunate in stumbling upon live oak as their primary source of fire fuel. Cedar was all around as well, but like green mesquite, it creates a bitter taste. Live oak is a hardwood and therefore very dense. It transfers the best type of heat for cooking as it packs more BTUs of potential heat energy per volume of firewood. Oak is great for its slow-burning characteristics as well as its small flame. Ideally, oak that is aged a year or two gives off a better flavor, but overall, cooking with this hardwood produces a light smoky flavor that works well for ribs, red meat, pork, and heavy game. Oak also burns clean, producing a light ash that doesn't coat the meat when it's cooking, which can make it taste gritty.

SALT LICK BRISKET

THE KEY to a great brisket is to cook it super low and super slow. We use a rub to start the brisket and then baste it once if not twice, which separates us from other barbecue places in Central Texas that don't use any sauce. We have more of a Southeastern influence on our barbecue, but not so much that what we serve isn't decidedly Texas barbecue. We use a sauce to help create a barrier between the meat and the heat to hold in all the juices.

Our sauce is vinegar and sugar–based. Many make the mistake of using tomato in their sauce, which only burns when you baste the meat, making a bitter flavor overall. Our sauce has a balanced blend of ingredients that allows the meat to caramelize nicely. It's not something that tastes burned, even though there is a black crust.

1 13- to 15-pound brisket *(14 pounds is the ideal weight that the Salt Lick uses, but you can adjust weight of brisket according to your needs. Our rule of thumb is to cook a brisket 75 minutes per pound of meat.)*
1 bottle favorite barbecue dry rub *(We recommend simple: salt, pepper, and something with heat.)*
1 bottle favorite barbecue basting sauce *(It should not have tomatoes but should be somewhat acidic and sugary to help caramelization.)*

NOTE: If you like your brisket a little crispier on the outside, simply baste the meat a little less during the smoking process. If you prefer your brisket more done, continue to cook in smoker, but remember, the longer you cook, the drier the meat.

Bring temperature of smoker to 225 degrees. (See page 191 for smoker instructions.) Rub entire brisket with dry rub until the meat is fully coated. In a closed smoker, place brisket on smoking rack fat-side down. Position brisket midway from the heat source to allow for a consistent cooking temperature. The deckle (thick end) should point to hotter part of heat source and the small end should be farthest away. Be sure to maintain the temperature at 225 degrees.

After 1 hour, inspect brisket. It should be gray, and seasoning should adhere to meat. There will be some caramelization of the ends and points. Baste brisket with sauce and reduce temperature to 185 degrees. Baste every 4 hours, giving special attention to end and points and any other area that appears to be scorching.

There are many factors that effect consistent heat for smoking meat, including the weather and the time of year. For that reason, you have to regularly check your meat temperature as you near the end of cooking. For a 14-pound brisket, it should take about 17½ hours to cook. Depending on the size of the brisket you select, we suggest checking the temperature of your brisket about 3 hours before the estimated cooking time is completed and every 30 minutes following. You want to make sure the heat is not cooking the brisket too quickly. If the internal temperature is nearing 165 degrees at the thickest part of the meat, you may need to remove the brisket earlier. Once the brisket has reached an internal temperature of 165-175 degrees (depending on your desired degree of doneness), it is ready for removal. Place brisket on the rack and let rest for at least 20 minutes before serving. The juices will continue to melt into the meat.

Brisket 101

AT THE SALT LICK, our cooking process for brisket involves five elements that all begin with an S: selection, seasoning, searing, slow cooking, and the sauce caramelization process. We'll go into each in more detail shortly, but first we're going to give you the brisket breakdown.

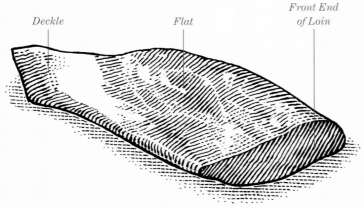

Deckle   *Flat*   *Front End of Loin*

FIG. 1 **THE BRISKET**

FIG. 2 **BEEF CUT DIAGRAM**

Brisket *is a cut of meat from the breast or lower chest of beef. The brisket muscles include the superficial and deep pectorals. As cattle do not have collar bones, those muscles support about 60 percent of the body weight of standing and moving cattle. That requires a significant amount of connective tissue, so the resulting meat must be cooked correctly to tenderize the connective tissue.*

The Loin: *This is the leanest muscle on a brisket. It will get done the quickest because it is thinner than the other muscles.*

The Flat: *This is a muscle that sits right on top of the loin. It has a little more fat, and the muscle sinews are a little larger. A portion of it gets carved with the loin once the brisket is being served, but the majority will be cut from the loin along with the deckle to cook and caramelize a little longer under the heat.*

The Deckle: *This is the back part of the brisket. It is where a lot of the "burnt ends" come from that people like so much these days. This portion also gets cooked a little longer on the heat than the loin.*

You can select a brisket anywhere from 5 pounds to 20 pounds. It really doesn't matter. For the most consistent cooking according to our specs, we recommend a 13- to 14-pound brisket.

This portion on the top of the brisket is what we refer to as the flat. It has a different muscle composition and is more marbled than the loin. Because it is a thicker piece of meat, we suggest cooking it a little longer once the loin has been cooked and removed.

These are the three separate muscles that make up a brisket: the loin, the flat, and the deckle. To cook, you leave those all intact. But we do suggest carving the flat and deckle off of the loin once the loin is completely cooked to let those two parts cook a little longer.

SELECTION

WHEN BUYING your brisket, ALWAYS buy USDA Choice meat or higher. If you buy a brisket that is 99 cents a pound rather than the more expensive $2.50 a pound, you've already started out on the wrong foot. All you're going to end up with is tough meat.

As my dad used to say, "If you start with a good piece of meat, you have a good chance of ending up with a good product. If you start with a bad piece of meat, you're going to end up with a worse product than what you began with."

I agree with him. If you're going to invest the time and effort in doing something like this, you might as well give yourself the best chance of succeeding from the beginning. That's what you do when you buy the Choice grade versus buying the cheap grade.

Always look at your brisket before you buy and be sure that the thickness in the loin is uniform across the front end. It should not be skinny at one end and thick at the other end. You'll just cook the meat unevenly.

Cook any size brisket you want, but the ideal weight for our cooking instructions is about 14 pounds.

The Meat Count

In one year, the Salt Lick uses:

80,000 pounds of turkey

110,000 pounds of chicken

125,000 pounds of sausage

550,000 pounds of pork ribs

950,000 pounds of brisket

SEASONING

To season brisket, you can play with different seasoning recipes. Some people just use salt and pepper. Others use a lot of spices. For the Salt Lick, we keep it to a simple three ingredients: salt, pepper, cayenne pepper. Now you can simply buy the rub at Texas area grocery stores, online, or at the Salt Lick restaurants. But when my dad was doing this years ago, he had a method that helped him make sure the quantities were just right.

Also, it's important that you WAIT to season your meat until your fire is ready. Once the meat is seasoned, you need to immediately put it on the fire. Otherwise the salt in the rub will begin to draw moisture from the meat. Salt your meat only when you are ready to put it on the fire.

[1] First, my dad would set out his brisket and three separate bowls with pepper, salt, and cayenne each. [2] Next, he would take the salt and sprinkle liberally all over the surface of the meat. [3] Then, he sprinkled an equal amount of pepper all over the brisket. [4] Finally, he would take just a pinch of the cayenne and sprinkle it in a single line down the center of the meat. [5] With his hands, he would rub the spices uniformly and firmly into the meat to make sure they adhered. [6] Flip the brisket and repeat the same steps on the other side. [7] A good tip to keep in mind is to always season the meat a little more than you think you need to. It is a big piece of meat and will take a lot of time to cook. You want to make sure those spices meld during the cooking process. [8] Make sure your meat is at room temperature before putting on the fire. This will help ensure a good sear. [9] Always season a little more than you think you need to.

SEARING AND SLOW COOKING

THIS IS WHERE the time and patience come in. You have to watch your meat, watch your smoker temperature, and watch your smoke. Whatever you do, always keep the thicker part of the meat closer to the heat source. It takes the longest to cook, and you want your thinner meat to cook in as uniform time as possible with the thicker part.

We like to sear our meat at a higher temperature first before letting it slow cook over the fire. When you fire up your smoker, get it to 225 degrees to begin the searing process. We sear the meat for 1 hour and then start the slow cooking process.

Once you begin slow cooking the meat, you will need to bring the temperature to 185 degrees. The rule of thumb is that it takes 75 minutes for each pound of meat that you are cooking. That's about 17 ½ hours total for a 14-pound brisket.

It is crucial that you wait to season your brisket just before you're ready to put it on the smoker to sear. Be sure the meat is also at room temperature.

Place your brisket on the smoker, being sure to place the thicker side (loin side) of the meat closer to the heat box and the deckle away from the heat.

Sear the meat at 225 degrees consistently for about an hour. The brisket should turn almost gray in color, and the seasoning should have really adhered to the meat.

Once the meat is seared, remove and bring the temperature of the smoker down to 195 degrees.

Replace brisket, meat-side up, baste for the first time with sauce, and let cook at that lower temperature. Baste every 4 hours, giving special attention to the end points.

About 3 hours before estimated cooking time is reached, check the brisket's internal temperature at the thickest part of the meat. Once the brisket has reached an internal temperature of 165-175 degrees (depending on your desired degree of doneness), it is ready for removal. If it isn't, check the temperature in 30-minute intervals.

SAUCE CARAMELIZATION PROCESS

A LOT OF Central Texas barbecue restaurants prefer to smoke their meats dry, without sauce. We choose to use sauce through the cooking process because it's a key part to layering flavor. Our sauce has a balanced sugar and acid content that does two things. First, it creates a moisture barrier between the meat and the radiant heat. The sauce caramelizes, which keeps the meat from drying out. Second, as the sauce caramelizes, it creates a second, smoky flavor component from flare-ups when it drips into the fire.

Once the meat has been seared, we begin the sauce caramelization process. This is what really brings a different flavor dimension to the brisket. Use a mop to drench the brisket in sauce as you begin the slow-cooking process.

The meat should be completely covered in sauce, even on the ends. At the restaurant we like to say that the meat has to be "shiny" on every square inch or it won't be as good. Then place it on the smoker with the thickest end toward the heat source.

At the Salt Lick, once the brisket is completely cooked, we sauce it again and put it directly over heat for a final caramelization. As the sauce drips onto the coals, more smoke billows up to add even more flavor. You can recreate this at home using a grill at really high heat.

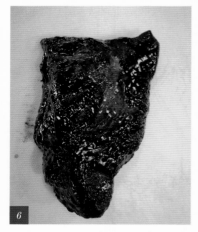

The brisket will eventually turn dark with the caramelized sauce, making a thick, crunchy crust on the exterior.

As we are caramelizing all of our meats on the open pit before serving, we move our briskets in a circuit around the pit based on where they are in the caramelization process and how we've carved the meat to order. That allows us to have the perfect brisket ready to serve at all times.

This is how a finished brisket should look. You can see that it has browned and crisped uniformly around the meat and that there is still a layer of "shiny" sauce that has cooked into it. Now you're ready to carve.

CARVING A BRISKET

ONCE YOU'VE PULLED your brisket off the fire, let it rest for 15 to 20 minutes to let the juices set back into the meat, or they'll end up on your plate. Begin carving with the fat side up. Remove the top fat portion to reveal a little less than ¼ inch of fat on the meat. That will allow you to see the grain of the meat so that you'll know where to carve. Always carve against the grain. If you carve the meat with the grain, it becomes stringy, loses its moisture, and gets really dry. Don't be afraid to remove the flat and the deckle from the loin and let them cook longer. The muscles are all different sizes. The loin will always be done quicker than the flat and the deckle. A lot of barbecue restaurants carve the whole brisket and serve it from front to back. While the flat and the deckle are usually done enough to serve, in our opinion, they're not really completely done enough to reveal their best flavor. They both still have fat that needs to be cooked out and flavor that needs to develop. We cook them all together until the loin is finished, and then we carve the loin up until we reach the flat. Then we cut off the flat and deckle and cook them a little longer on the heat source to achieve a better flavor.

This is an example to show the difference in the brisket you start out with and the brisket you end up with. You can see how much the meat shrinks once the fat has been cooked out of it.

To begin carving, place the brisket on a cutting board with the fat side facing up. This way you can trim away the fat before you get into carving the meat.

Remove the fat portion to reveal a little less than ½ inch of fat on the meat. That will allow you to see the grain of the meat so that you'll know where to carve.

Slice the fat off, but be careful not to cut into the meat. You should be able to feel the difference with your knife.

When you get to the very corner, you'll find the end is more meat than fat and is black and crispy. This is a "burnt end," or what we like to call "brisket tenderloin"—it's the best part. Trim that and set aside for serving to your most deserving friends or family. (Or just keep for yourself.)

Always carve against the grain. If you carve the meat with the grain, it becomes stringy, loses its moisture, and gets really dry. First you will be cutting into the brisket loin. Carve that up to the point that you begin to reach the flat.

Once you've sliced the brisket loin to the flat, we like to separate the flat and the deckle from the rest of the loin and let them continue to cook on the open pit. You don't have to. In fact, a lot of other restaurants carve the whole thing together. But we prefer to do it this way.

In our opinion, the flat and deckle are not really completely done enough to reveal their best flavor. They both still have fat that needs to be cooked out and flavor that needs to develop.

Once you have removed the flat and deckle, you are left with a perfectly cooked brisket loin. Continue to carve it against the grain and serve.

The area around the flat and deckle has a lot of fat. It's best to trim that off and discard before you put them back on the fire.

Once the flat and deckle have been trimmed of fat, baste again with sauce and put them back on the fire for at least 15 to 20 more minutes each.

We used to trim our meat to get rid of almost all of the fat. That's when people were worried about too much fat. Now people like fat because they think it adds flavor. The customer is always right. So we adjust our brisket trim as food trends dictate.

This is to show the three separate parts of the brisket before they are cooked and after. You can see that separately they are all very different types of meat.

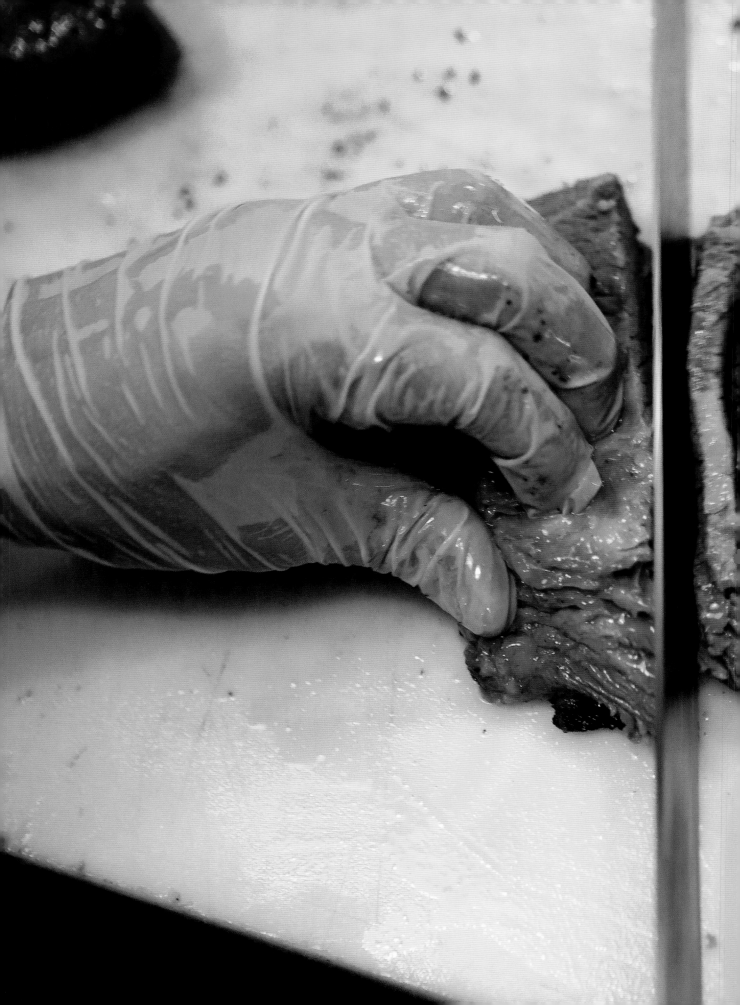

SALT LICK SAUSAGE

THE SALT LICK serves a fully cooked sausage made especially for the restaurant by J Bar B Foods out of Waelder, Texas. J Bar B specializes in sausage and specialty meats and has been making our sausage for more than 30 years. We used a different purveyor when my father was running the restaurant. But one day, I was manning the pit and a guy walked up to me and asked me to sample his sausage. He was wearing a pair of thick glasses and looked a lot like Buddy Holly. We started a conversation, and I really liked him—his sausage was good too. I shared some with my father later that day. He didn't like it as much as the sausage we were already using, but I told him I thought the customers would really like it and that I just liked the guy and wanted to help him out. We've been buying our sausage from the company he worked for ever since.

You can make sausage out of just about any kind of meat. Beef, chicken, lamb, turkey. But there is one truism about sausage: You can always make it better by adding pork. We use a beef and pork blend. The key to serving good sausage is to serve it hot. You want the fat in the sausage to melt so that it moves throughout the whole link. When you're cooking it and the juice starts to burst from the casing in little geysers, it's ready to serve. Some sausage from other barbecue restaurants leaves a greasy coating in your mouth. Serving it really hot prevents that, as does using a finer grind of meat.

You can use links from any reputable butcher or meat purveyor in your area. Simply bring the sausage to an internal temperature of 140 degrees over a smoker before serving. *NOTE: It is important that you reach an internal temperature of 140 degrees in two hours, otherwise the flavor is off.*

How to Cope with the Meat Sweats

If you've ever overindulged on a feast of barbecue, steak, or any other fantastic meal with meat, then you know what the "meat sweats" are. The symptoms are unmistakable: sweating, drowsiness, delirium, indigestion, bloating, and the urge to curl up on the nearest couch and fall asleep.

Apparently, the increased amounts of adrenaline combined with the excess protein cause the body to increase in temperature and subsequently cause you to sweat... profusely. It's sometimes referred to as a food coma, which is the completely natural feeling of fatigue you get when you've finished eating a large meal. As a general rule of thumb, the bigger the meal, the bigger the food coma.

But there's no need to panic. You can always pop a couple of antacids or get up and try to move around to settle your stomach. I've heard a little Alka Seltzer is helpful too. But the only true remedy for the meat sweats is to take a nap.

We always keep a wheelbarrow out back and will happily accommodate you by wheeling you back to your car. Or, if you have the time, we can wheel you straight to our hammock grove, in our nearby beer garden, and you can doze off your ailment beneath the shade of oak trees.

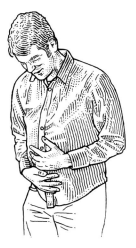

SAUSAGE HOW-TO:
[1] To begin our process of preparing sausage, we bring out the links from refrigeration and hang them on hooks above the open pit. That brings them to room temperature so the meat isn't immediately shocked when we put it directly on the heat. That also allows smoke to infuse into the meat. You can do the same by placing sausage links in the smoker away from the heat source but where they can absorb the smoke. [2] Once the sausage has been brought up to a warm temperature, we put it directly over the fire. At home, simply do the same on your grill. [3] Not all barbecue restaurant sausage is the same. Sometimes when you taste it, it leaves a greasy coating in your mouth. That is because it hasn't been cooked properly. When you cook sausage, get enough heat in it so that the fat breaks down and creates juices flowing through the meat. You'll know it is done when the casing begins to blister and burst. [4] You should see juice flowing from the sausage at the same time. At that point, the sausage is done and it must be served and eaten immediately.

SALT LICK PORK RIBS

THERE ARE two schools of thought for cooking pork ribs. Either cook them slow or cook them fast. We cook our ribs as fast as we can. Unlike briskets, ribs are not a thick, heavily marbled piece of meat. The longer you leave them in a hot, smoky environment, the greater the chance that they will lose their moisture and dry out. When you cook them fast, you keep that moisture, which gives the meat more flavor.

We use spare ribs at the Salt Lick. It's the more traditional way to serve pork ribs, and they have both a baby back rib appeal and an additional meatier brisket side. It's sort of like a T-bone steak. You get the best of both worlds with different flavors. Baby back ribs became more trendy in recent years, and we serve them on Sundays, but my personal favorite are spare ribs.

I used to stand beside the pit and eat a whole rack at a time. In fact, one of my favorite memories of eating at the Salt Lick was after working all morning with our ranch hand, Lupe, on a wooden fence. We came in for lunch, and I polished off a whole rack of those ribs with a few cherry peppers on the side. I was looking at grabbing a few more, when my dad got my attention and said, "Hey, stop eating the ribs! You need to save some for the customers!"

For this recipe, you can use baby back ribs, but they are thinner and leaner than spare ribs, so you need to adjust the amount of sauce and time accordingly (generally less for both). A lot of people like the meat to "fall off the bone." When it comes to ribs, we feel that the meat is perfect just before it gets there. The meat should pull back just a little bit when you bite it and then come clean off the bone. When it is so tender that it falls off the bone with little effort, the meat is too done.

For spare ribs, it's important to keep the brisket end (thicker end) closer to the heat source while smoking and put the leaner rib end away from the heat source. You will know the ribs are done when the meat has pulled away from the bone by about ¼ inch. You can also use a fork to see if it moves around easily on the thick part of the ribs.

SPARE RIBS VS.
BABY BACK RIBS

When it comes to barbecue ribs, you can use either spare ribs or baby back ribs. We chose to use spare ribs at the Salt Lick, but the principles are essentially the same. Keep in mind that baby back ribs are not as meaty or thick as spare ribs, so you need to pay attention as you cook them. They will cook a lot faster than spare ribs.

1 bottle favorite barbecue dry rub
1 bottle favorite barbecue basting sauce (one without tomatoes in it)
1 rack of spare or baby back ribs

Bring smoker to 250 degrees. Uniformly spread dry rub on front and back of ribs and place on smoker meat-side down. Close door, and cook for 1 hour. Baste ribs with barbecue sauce. Turn the ribs over, meat-side up, and baste again, giving great care to basting ends and caramelized areas.

Cook for 2 more hours and check internal temperature. If the ribs have reached 160 degrees, remove. If not, cook for an additional 15 minutes and continue to check in 15-minute intervals until temperature reaches 160 degrees. Remove and place on wire cooling rack on sheet pan meat-side up to rest. Let rest at least 15 minutes before serving.

[1] When selecting pork ribs, the key is to make sure there are no "shiners" or "moons," which are bones protruding from the meat. The meat should still completely encase the bone. Otherwise the finished product will be dry. [2] A lot of people like to remove the thin membrane that covers the interior of the ribs before they cook it. That is fine if you are using a slow-cook method. But because we cook our ribs fast and at a hotter temperature, the membrane cooks off. You don't need to remove it unless you just want to make extra work for yourself. [3] Along the center of the ribs is a long, thin strip of meat and membrane. It's what many people refer to as the "skirt" or "fajita" of the pork rib. [4] Before you season your meat, you need to remove the fajita. Otherwise it will make your cooking uneven in that particular spot. [5] Along the thicker end of the rib is the "brisket bone." It's a really hard bone that runs in a different pattern from the rest of the ribs. Even though it has decent meat on it, it's an awkward piece to have to cut when you're serving up ribs and should be removed. [6] Before we season the meat, we cut off the brisket bone and save it for cooking in our pinto beans for added flavor, just as you would chicken bones for chicken stock.

[7] This may seem like common sense, but you'd be surprised at how many people put the wrong end of the ribs near the heat source of the grill or smoker. They end up with one side of overcooked meat and another side of undercooked meat. [8] For even cooking, it's crucial to keep the thicker end of the ribs pointed toward the heat source. That helps protect the thinner end from overcooking and drying out.

THE PERFECT DONENESS
You can always use a heat thermometer to gauge the temperature of your meat, but there are really two easier ways to tell when your ribs are ready. You will know the ribs are done when the meat has pulled away from the top of the bone by about ¼ inch. You can also use a fork to see if it moves around easily on the thick part of the ribs. If so, your ribs are done.

FALL OFF THE BONE?
Despite the common wisdom that meat should be so tender that it falls off the bone, that's not the correct logic for pork ribs. We think the meat is too done if it's to the point that it falls off the bone. What you're looking for is a little give in the meat when you bite into it. It should pull back just a little bit and then come clean off the bone. That's when you know the meat is perfectly done.

SALT LICK BEEF RIBS

THOUGH PORK RIBS are more often associated with barbecue, beef ribs are a quintessential part of the Texas barbecue family. Quite a bit larger than pork spare ribs, beef ribs are sold as one per order. We sell them as a "double cut" by butchering out every other bone so that you get double the meat in your order. They're rich and smoky and one of the best cuts of beef you'll ever put in your mouth. We've had a number of celebrity chefs come here throughout the years, and the beef ribs have always been a big hit.

"Here is the real deal. I eat a ton of those Salt Lick beef ribs," said Food Network chef Bobby Flay on one of his visits to the restaurant. "They are fantastic! Lots of flavor! Salt Lick makes its own barbecue rules. It is so good. Beef ribs are something I don't usually cook. It is something I leave to the Salt Lick."

1 rack beef back ribs
1 bottle favorite dry rub
1 bottle favorite barbecue basting sauce (one without tomatoes in it)

Heat smoker to 225 degrees. Remove skin from back of bone side of ribs and discard. Rub each rack of ribs with dry rub for a moderately heavy coating. Place ribs meat-side down on rack of closed smoker midway from the main heat source. Cook ½ hour. Lightly baste each rack with Salt Lick Bar-B-Que Sauce, then turn over and baste meat side. Let temperature of smoker cool to 180 degrees. Baste every 1½ hours for a total cook time of 6½ hours. Check internal temperature of ribs in center of rack, making sure thermometer is not touching bone. If temperature is 160 degrees, ribs are ready for removal. If not, monitor temperature every 15 minutes, until ribs have reached 160 degrees. Remove to wire cooling rack on flat sheet pan. Baste ribs once more, and separate individual ribs with sharp knife. Serve immediately.

Generations of Flavor

Every generation of our family has contributed a little tweak or two to the way we do barbecue. It's evolved from my great grandmother, Bettie, digging makeshift earth berms on the wagon trail to my grandmother, Roxie, hosting the family at her home for a full day of butchering and smoking a whole hog and my father perfecting the things he learned from them to create the barbecue. Of course, he added a few tweaks of his own.

He originally used pecan wood that he sourced from our property, but when he ran out of that, he found that live oak actually worked even better. (He still used pecan hulls to add a little bit of that pecan flavor back into the smoke.) He also began cooking our meats in a two-method process. Instead of smoking and serving the barbecue immediately, he found that things always seems to taste better on the second day. The flavors melded together and tasted even better after they had had time to sit for a while. So he fashioned a way to smoke and cook the meat, bring it down to a cold temperature quickly, and hold things overnight. The next day, he would bring the meats back up to temperature on the open pit and serve them directly to the customer. The difference in flavor was amazing. And it's something we continue to do to this very day.

My mother also added a couple of tweaks. She added toasted sesame and celery seeds to the coleslaw for more texture and flavor. She also added a little bit of ginger to my father's barbecue sauce, which is one of the ingredients that makes it such a uniquely delicious sauce today.

People often ask me what I plan to tweak with the barbecue. I'm here to say that I like what the generations before me have done to get the Salt Lick to where it is today. In my opinion, if it ain't broke, don't fix it. So this old boy isn't changing a thing.

Jaime, Carmen, and Robert Gonzales.

A Family of Pit Masters

★ ★ ★

CARMEN GONZALES

My name is Carmen Gonzales. I started working for Mr. Thurman Roberts about 40 years ago, when I was 18 years old, I think. I was with him when he first opened the restaurant, and I've done everything from mop floors to make potato salad. But mainly I've been what most people call the "pit master." When I learned to cook barbecue, it was Mr. Thurman and Scott who took their time with me and showed me how to do it right.

I'm originally from Guanajato, Mexico, but I came to the United States when I was 16. I've worked for the Salt Lick almost my entire life in America. When it was open only for a few days a week, I worked another job too, making concrete and cement, but eventually I just worked here all the time. When Mr. Thurman had the pecan house, I would help them clean and shell the pecans, and then I'd come to the pit on weekends to watch over the barbecue.

Sometimes I worked all night. I had a little cot and a place I could sleep. It meant I wasn't home with my family, but it was part of the job at the beginning. After the restaurant grew, I didn't have to work as many hours. Over the years, I would hang out with a lot of the other Salt Lick staff. They were white people, no Spanish-speaking people. For the longest time, I was the only Mexican. But everyone was always so nice, and I learned to speak English. Over the years my brother has come to work here on the grounds crew and a number of my cousins as well.

Forty-three years is a long time to stay at the same job, but I stayed here because I liked it. I've been asked by other places to come cook barbecue for them, but I've never even considered it. Other places don't cook barbecue the same way we do. But more than that, the Roberts family has always been so great to me. Mr. Thurman and Scott taught me everything I know about making great barbecue. And it's a place where I've been able to raise my family.

People ask me all the time what it takes to make really good barbecue. The first answer is time. You can't rush good barbecue. You have to let it make itself. Other than that, what makes the Salt Lick great barbecue is the sauce. And the wood. And the rub. And the cook. But mainly the sauce. Not everyone uses sauce for their barbecue, but it's one thing that really sets our food apart. The spices and flavor that it adds to the meat while it's cooking are what make it good. The important thing is to keep your eye on everything. The heat, the coals, the smoke, and, most importantly, the meat.

I never really thought I'd be a cook when I was younger, but I love what I do. You can't do this job and not love it. It comes through in the barbecue. Before Mr. Thurman passed away, he asked me, "Carmen, how long are you going to stay here with me?" I told him I didn't know but that I had no plans to leave. Since then, I made a promise to him and Scott that I would stay until they no longer needed me. Over the years, the restaurant has gotten bigger and more people come now than ever before. But we have figured out a way to time everything perfectly, even though we're making a whole lot more barbecue in one day than we used to make in one week.

When my first son, Jaime, was old enough, I got him a job here and began teaching him how to do everything. Now he's the No. 2 pit master. My second son, Robert, is next in line. Right now he's learning how to work in other parts of the restaurant, but it won't be long before we start teaching him how to work with the meat.

JAIME AND ROBERT GONZALES

Jaime: I started coming to the Salt Lick when I was just a little kid. On my dad's days off, he brought me up there to show me around and check on things. I came out there a lot when I was growing up. I learned how to work in the back of the restaurant and how to do some of the groundswork around the property. In the parking lot, I even learned how to drive a car. In 1997 I came to work there full time. I was only 16. I had to start from the ground up and learn the different stations in the kitchen. Back then, we still used only open pits for smoking the meats. It wasn't until 1999 that we brought in the rotisserie smokers to begin the smoking process.

My dad is right. You have to love what you're doing there. If you don't, you're not going to do a good job. And it's not something you really grow to love. You have to have a heart for it from the beginning. It gets hot around the pits, especially in the summer. And you have to manage smoke always getting in your eyes. Most importantly, you have to be consistent in getting all the meat just right. That's not easy.

People come in to train, and I've seen their eyes start to wander off or they get impatient with what they're being taught, and I know they're not going to stick around. It's not as easy as people think.

Robert: When you grow up eating this barbecue like I have, it's almost in your blood that one day you'll get to make it yourself. I started working at the Salt Lick when I was 16, in 1999, and worked my way through the stations like my brother did. My dad and Jaime both have their little secrets for how they get the meat just right. I'm just starting to learn what they know, and I'm sure I'll have a few secrets of my own before too long. I spent a lot of time working as a waiter and at the cutting table. Those are two areas I've mastered. Over the next couple of years, I want to master the pit, but my dad and brother say it will take a while before they trust me with it completely.

Jaime: The biggest difference I've noticed over the years is in the amount of food we're having to put out, which means we have to stay organized. The other change I've noticed are the people who come here. For a long time we had a lot of college students from San Marcos and Austin. They'd come out here and bring their own beer and have a good time. When there were big football games, they'd always come out here. We still see that today, but we see a lot more families come with their children. And there's more diversity. A lot of people come from outside of Texas.

Robert: Yeah, they do come from all over the world. Every day I talk to people from Australia, people from Germany, people from Puerto Rico or Mexico. They come from all over the world. I love working in the front of the house for that reason. You just get to meet so many people, and they're all so excited to be there.

Jaime: There are a lot of other barbecue places in Texas. And a lot of other styles of barbecue. But I like ours the best. I live in Lockhart, where some of the top barbecue joints are. They're good, but there's no comparison to what the Salt Lick does. That's why I work here and not there.

Robert: I agree with that. There is no comparison. Other barbecue places do things in their own style. A lot of them don't even use sauce. They just use a rub, and they stick to a certain tradition. But since we do use sauce, it changes the kind of barbecue we serve. But more than that, working at the Salt Lick is like working with one big family. There's a dedication and tradition that has been built on the fact that everyone has worked there for so long. That's what draws people to come and experience it.

Jamie: That's true—it's about the people. The owners are really nice. A lot of other places just treat the process like it's a robot. Here, I know I'm trusted to be in charge of what I do. That's what makes you care about doing a great job every day. People come in all the time and say things to me like, "Oh, my God, I can't believe how good this is. How do you do it?" My answer is that it's not so much about all the little things I do to turn out good barbecue. It's about how much I love what I do, and that's what comes out in the food that you eat.

People always want to know the secret ingredient to great barbecue. At the Salt Lick, it's the people you see here. Without this dedicated staff, the smiles on our customers' faces would be a lot smaller.

SALT LICK SMOKED TURKEY

SMOKED TURKEY hasn't always been on our menu. But as times have changed and people are thinking more about the health of their heart and their waistlines, we decided to offer something that would appeal to those sensibilities—but we made sure to give it a little Salt Lick flare as well. For the best results, brine the turkey a day in advance. It helps to increase the moistness of the meat. For flavor, we rely on the turkey smoke and the Salt Lick Bar-B-Que Sauce.

    1 12-pound turkey breast
    1 bottle favorite barbecue sauce

    Poultry brine ingredients:
    1½ gallons water
    1 cup sugar
    ½ cup salt

Mix well. Rinse turkey and pat dry. Seal in a large container with poultry brine, and place in refrigerator for 24 hours. Bring smoker to 265 degrees. When ready to smoke, rinse turkey with cold water and pat dry. Baste turkey well with Salt Lick Bar-B-Que Sauce. Place on smoker rack midway from heat source.

Baste turkey after 3 hours. At 5½ hours, check internal temperature of turkey at thickest area of the breast. If the temperature is 165 degrees, turkey breast is ready for removal. If temperature is not 165 degrees, recheck in 15-minute intervals. Remove from smoker and place on a sheet pan to rest. Baste turkey before slicing and serving.

Chicken and the Salt Lick

Out of deference to my father, I'm leaving out the smoked chicken recipe from the Salt Lick. My dad served brisket, ribs, and sausage when he ran the restaurant. He said if the Salt Lick ever sold chicken, it would be over his dead body. In his mind, it just wasn't barbecue. But as times changed and people wanted other options, we had to adjust our perspective. We added habenero-glazed chicken to our menu that includes a few bastings of Lauren's Spicy Recipe Bar-B-Que Sauce. It may not have been my father's preference, but we sell more than 100,000 pounds of chicken each year. I guess he wasn't right about everything.

SMOKING ON A WEBER GRILL:
[1-2] Using a charcoal grill such as a Weber, prepare a charcoal pyramid in the center of the grill, leaving room around the outer circle for the chicken to cook with indirect heat. Light the fire and let burn until all of the coals are white on the outside. [3] Cut two chickens in half and bring to room temperature. Just before you are ready to place on the grill, season liberally with Salt Lick Dry Rub, or dry rub of your choice. [4] It is key that you wait to season the chicken until you are ready to put it on the fire. Otherwise, the salt will draw moisture out of the meat.

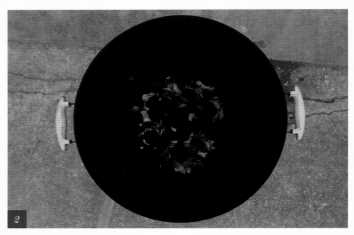

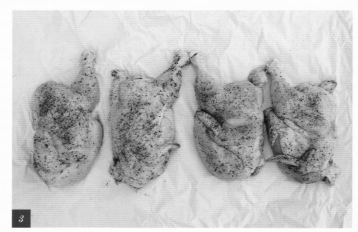

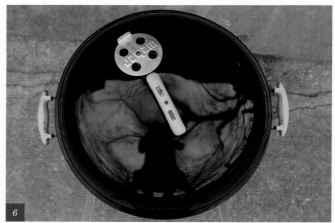

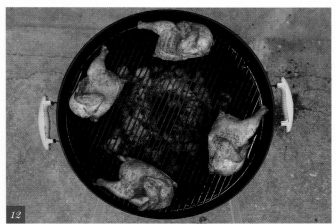

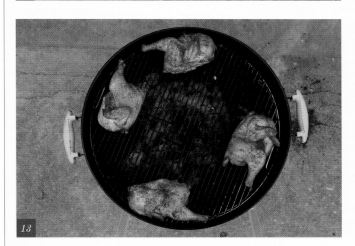

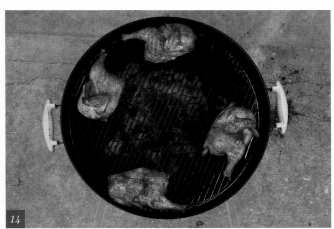

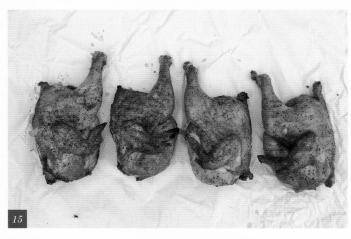

[5] Grease the grill grate to prevent meat from sticking, and arrange the chickens equidistant from each other around the outer circle of the grill. Make sure the skin side is facing up and the back of the chicken is facing the fire. [6] Cover the chicken with the lid and let cook for 15 minutes. [7-11] Remove the lid and rotate each chicken so that the breast is toward the flames. Replace the lid and cook for 15 more minutes. [12] Repeat the process of rotating the chicken front and back every 15 minutes for up to 45 minutes total. [13] Remove the lid only to rotate the chicken. You will notice the chicken becomes darker on the exterior. [14] For the last 5 to 10 minutes, open the vent on the grill lid to allow the air flow to crisp the chicken skin. [15] Remove chicken and let rest for 10 to 15 minutes before serving.

SALT LICK PRIME RIB WITH
JALAPEÑO-TOMATILLO HORSERADISH SAUCE

ON SUNDAYS, we offer a special menu item: prime rib. It's a bit of an indulgence for the meat lover in all of us, particularly popular for Father's Day. We tend to run out before noon. We use a bone-in prime rib. The flavor of prime rib is superior if cooked on the bone. For this recipe, the garlic salt and smoke combine to make an amazing flavor.

1 10-pound prime rib roast
Garlic salt

Heat smoker to 225 degrees. Evenly season (medium heavy) prime rib with garlic salt. Place rib on smoking rack midway from heat source. DO NOT baste prime ribs. Smoke for 2 hours. Check internal temperature at thickest part of prime rib, targeting 125 degrees. If it has not reached 125 degrees, check in 15-minute intervals until temperature is reached. Remove prime ribs from smoker and place on wire rack, bone-side down. Serve with jalapeño-tomatillo horseradish sauce.

Jalapeño-Tomatillo Horseradish Sauce:
12 tomatillos, husked and washed
1 large red onion, coarsely chopped
4 cloves garlic, chopped
2 jalapeños, chopped
2 tablespoons canola oil
Salt and freshly ground black pepper
3 tablespoons rice vinegar
¼ cup prepared horseradish, drained
¼ cup chopped fresh cilantro leaves

Preheat oven to 350 degrees. Place tomatillos, onion, garlic, and jalapeño in medium roasting pan, toss with oil, and season. Cook until mixture is soft, but do not allow it to color, 20 to 25 minutes. Transfer to food processor, and process until smooth. Add vinegar, horseradish, and cilantro, and pulse just to combine. Season with salt and pepper. Scrape into bowl, cover, and refrigerate for at least 1 hour before serving.

This could easily be considered one of the manliest cuts of meat out there. And we do our best to serve it up in good Texas barbecue fashion. It's no surprise it's a big seller on Father's Day.

3,500
BY THE NUMBERS
For holidays such as Father's Day, the Salt Lick serves up to 3,500 people.

SALT LICK COLESLAW

THE SALT LICK coleslaw is a shredded cabbage salad mixed with vinegar and oil dressing. Dousing the cabbage with mayonnaise wasn't an option for settlers when they were traveling west in wagon trains. They had to use ingredients that wouldn't spoil. We wanted to stay as true as possible to how my family originally made coleslaw.

The key to this coleslaw is to mix and serve it fresh. Over time, the vinegar pulls juices from the cabbage, changing the texture, taste, and bite. At the restaurant, we don't make a batch of coleslaw until the first customer of the day has walked in the door. And we don't make another batch until the first tray is more than one quarter empty. That way we're constantly serving this classic salad at its absolute best.

Salt Lick vinegar mix:
1 cup white vinegar
¼ pound sugar
½ cup salt
¼ cup white pepper

1 head shredded cabbage
⅛ cup vegetable oil
Pinch celery seed
1 ounce sesame seeds, popped (toasted)
⅛ cup Salt Lick vinegar mix

For the Salt Lick vinegar mix: Place vinegar in heavy saucepan and bring to a boil. While vinegar is boiling, slowly add sugar and salt, stirring constantly until dissolved. Turn off heat. In mixing bowl, place white pepper. Slowly pour vinegar mixture into white pepper while whisking, and mix well. Cover.

For the coleslaw: Place cabbage in large mixing bowl. Sprinkle oil over top and mix thoroughly. Sprinkle celery seed and sesame seeds over top of cabbage, and mix thoroughly. Add Salt Lick vinegar mix, and combine well. Place in serving bowl, scrape all remaining seeds and dressing from mixing bowl, and add to serving bowl. Serve immediately because coleslaw is best served while cabbage is crisp and crunchy.

NOTE: This mixture can be refrigerated for up to 24 hours prior to making coleslaw. Be sure to mix well and have pepper in suspension prior to using in coleslaw dish.

It's All in the Cabbage Patch

Cabbage can vary in density depending on the time of year. In the wintertime, it has more water in it. The sauce used in this recipe will draw that water out more quickly, dampening the overall flavor. The best way to enjoy our coleslaw is to serve it and eat it immediately. It's really the best way to enjoy all of our food. In fact, in the sequence from serving bowl, to plate, to mouth, we suggest you just skip the plate.

SALT LICK POTATO SALAD

THE STAR of Salt Lick potato salad is the potato. Our salad is a simple mixture designed to enhance the flavor of the potato and complement the smoky taste of our meats. Unlike many potato salad recipes, ours keeps the jackets on the potatoes when we cook them. That keeps them dry. The hot, dry potato absorbs flavors easier because the pores are empty and large to absorb flavors in the sauces. With a cold, wet potato stock, the flavors and sauces coat only the outside of the potato. Potato salad must be kept as fresh as possible. *NOTE: The dry ingredients are mixed two times in order to ensure even distribution. The dry ingredients must be mixed prior to the addition of the wet ingredients. Otherwise, the potato salad will have an uneven distribution of flavors.*

NOTE: The Salt Lick uses a dry potato for our potato salad. Great emphasis is given to keeping the cooked potato as dry as possible. The closest comparison for the finished stock would be perfectly cooked baked potatoes peeled whole and then cubed.

Pickled onions:
1 medium yellow onion, diced
White vinegar, enough to coat onion in a bowl

4 large russet potatoes
Salt and pepper to taste
1 to 2 tablespoons sesame seeds, popped (toasted)
2 to 3 tablespoons diced pickled onion
½ cup Salt Lick Original Recipe Bar-B-Que Sauce

For the pickled onion: Place diced onion in small or medium bowl and cover with white vinegar. Place in the refrigerator for 24 hours, checking to make sure onions are submerged at all times. Reserve for potato salad.

For the potato salad: Wash potatoes and place in large pot. Do not peel potatoes. They need to cook in their jackets. Fill with water so at least 1 inch covers potatoes. Bring to a boil and cover. Cook, replenishing water as necessary, until a knife is easily inserted into center of potato. Carefully remove all hot water, leave potatoes in pan, and replace lid.

Prepare an ice bath in a medium bowl. Remove one potato from pan and replace cover. Quickly dip potato into ice water, remove, and peel. (Dipping the hot potato loosens the skin and makes it easier to peel.) Do not let potatoes soak in ice water as the potato needs to be dry while mixing. Repeat with remaining potatoes and chop into ¼-inch cubes. If you have excessive crumbling, that is okay because that is what will bind the potato salad together.

In a large bowl, sprinkle salt, pepper, and sesame seeds onto potatoes, and mix until well blended. Squeeze excess liquid from pickled onions. Sprinkle 2 to 3 tablespoons onions over potatoes, and blend well. Drizzle barbecue sauce over potatoes and add more sesame seeds, salt, and pepper to taste. Serve immediately. Serves 6 to 8.

SALT LICK PINTO BEANS

THE RECIPE for Salt Lick pinto beans originated over wood fires on wagon trains. The recipe relies on the flavor of the pinto beans enhanced by the flavors of chili dulce, comino, garlic, and salt. The secret ingredient is pork.

Salt Lick pinto beans are like chili. They always taste better on the second day. That's why we quick-chill our beans and then bring them back to temperature the following day to serve. The addition of butter during the re-temping process rounds out the flavor. The final product is an even mixture of beans and juice. That will require regular attention and stirring. *NOTE: The smallest amount of burned beans will require you to discard the entire batch.*

Too often you can get pinto beans that are soupy and nondescript in flavor. In our opinion, good pinto beans are as much a part of the real barbecue experience as brisket, ribs, and sausage. Because of that, we make sure our beans—and the rest of our sides, for that matter—get as much attention as everything else. You can taste the difference in the first bite.

Bean spice mix ingredients:
½ cup chili powder
¼ cup salt
1 tablespoon of granulated garlic
½ tablespoon oregano
½ tablespoon cumin

1 pound dried pinto beans
8 cups water
2 ounces pork butt
¼ cup of Salt Lick Bean Spice mix

Combine all bean spice ingredients and mix well.

Place beans on a flat surface and remove all rocks, dirt, debris, and broken or deformed beans. Place beans in colander and wash. Place in large heavy metal pot (cast-iron is preferable). Add enough water to cover beans by 1 inch. Bring to a boil, cover, turn off heat, and let beans sit for 1 hour. Add remaining ingredients, bring to a boil, reduce heat to a slow simmer, replace lid, and let beans cook for 1½ hours or until beans are tender.

Place container of beans in refrigerator for 24 hours. For the first 4 hours, cover ½ of the pot, and after the first 2 hours, stir. Replace lid halfway and cool for remaining 2 hours before fully covering. That will allow the beans to chill properly and uniformly.

NOTE: Only distilled or boiled water may be added to pinto beans during re-temping process. Tap water will cause the pinto beans to spoil. Stirring utensils should be wiped clean, not rinsed in tap water.

Re-temping Salt Lick Pinto Beans:
¼ cup water
2 tablespoons butter

Remove beans from refrigeration. If beans are dry, remove from pot to bowl, and add ¼ cup of water to pot, bring to a boil, and place beans back in pot. Bring beans to a boil, stirring frequently for up to 30 minutes. If beans begin to dry out, add boiling (not cold) water as necessary. After 30 minutes, reduce temperature to low simmer and stir in 2 tablespoons butter. Serve immediately.

SALT LICK PICKLED JALAPEÑOS

SALT LICK JALAPEÑOS are fresh and cold-pickled with a sweet pickle recipe. Cold pickling retains the color and bite of a fresh jalapeño much better than hot pickling. The hot pickle cooks the jalapeño, changing the color and making the texture softer. The Salt Lick is making a pickle jalapeño that resembles a fresh jalapeño as much as possible.

1½ pounds jalapeños
½ gallon white vinegar
½ cup white sugar
½ cup salt
¼ teaspoon ground oregano
1 large carrot
¼ large white onion
3 dried bay leaves
1 tablespoon whole black peppercorns

Wash jalapeños and drain until dry. In a 1-gallon bucket, stir together vinegar, sugar, salt, and oregano. Cut half of carrot into ¼-inch rounds and half into ¼-inch sticks approximately 3 inches long. Cut onion into 4 quarters. Add vegetables, bay leaves, and black peppercorns to vinegar mixture. Stir. To ensure jalapeños are submerged in liquid, place a plastic plate with a small plastic bowl on top of the mixture, then cover with lid.

Jalapeños vary in heat; it's just part of the breed. As the growing season moves along, the jalapeño plant blooms multiple times. Each time it blooms, the peppers get hotter. So sometimes you'll have peppers that are as mild as bell peppers, and other times they're hotter than hell.

NOTE: Never try to drink cold water to dampen the heat of a jalapeño once you eat one. That will only spread the oil in your mouth. Instead, drink a glass of milk. The basic quality of the milk will kill the acid in the pepper oil. If milk doesn't work, try butter instead.

SALT LICK PEACH COBBLER

THERE ARE FOUR families who have been in the Driftwood area for more than 100 years: the Howards, the Robertses, the Eckolses, and the Halls. Somehow I'm related to all four. The recipe for our peach cobbler sparked a debate between ladies from two of those families, Mrs. Eckols and Mrs. Hall. For a long time, we served only my dad's pecan pie at the restaurant, but after personally hand rolling and making 144 pecan pies one day, I said, "Enough is enough. We need an alternative that's a lot less labor intensive."

I decided to do cobbler. Peach cobbler. I love the peaches that come from the Hill Country in summertime. The dessert is the perfect way to finish off a barbecue feast. Of course, once Mrs. Eckols and Mrs. Hall tasted it for the first time, the debate broke out over whose recipe I had stolen. They each swore that I stole their cobbler recipe from them. Well, they're both wrong. I didn't steal Mrs. Eckols' recipe over Mrs. Hall's or vice versa. The truth is, I stole it from both of them and added a couple of tweaks of my own.

This cobbler is unique from other recipes in that it does not have a pastry laid on top of the fruit before baking. The cobbler dough we use begins at the bottom of the pan and rises up while baking to make a fruit and pastry topping. While it's cooking, the dough melds with the fruit filling and takes on all the flavors, including a delicious buttery taste. Butter and peaches work well together. In fact, if pork is the key ingredient to good sausage and beans, butter is the magical ingredient for baking, especially with this cobbler.

The cinnamon is kept to a minimum because it hides the taste of the peach. On the other hand, vanilla extract is used to heighten the natural flavor of the peach.

For the batter:
1 cup flour
¾ cup sugar
½ tablespoon baking powder
1 egg
1½ ounces evaporated milk
4 ounces water
2 ounces melted butter

Preheat oven to 375 degrees. In a bowl, mix first 3 ingredients. In another bowl, whisk together eggs, evaporated milk, and water. Add wet ingredients to dry, and mix to form a batter. Ladle butter to coat bottom and sides of 9 x 13–inch baking dish. Ladle batter onto butter, spread evenly, but do not mix.

For the peach filling:
3 pounds fresh peaches, or frozen, thawed
½ teaspoon vanilla extract
½ teaspoon fresh lemon juice
Pinch nutmeg
Pinch clove
2 pinches cinnamon
½ cup sugar
¾ cup water

In a bowl, mix together all ingredients, adding water last. Spread mixture evenly over batter, being careful not to mix the two. Bake for 15 minutes. Reduce heat to 350 degrees, and bake 45 to 50 minutes more, until done.

SALT LICK BLACKBERRY COBBLER

AFTER I TOOK over the restaurant operations, I wanted to bring back a dewberry cobbler that my grandmother, Roxie, used to make. Dewberries would come into season once a year, and she'd make the best cobbler I've ever had using those berries. I thought it would be great to use a berry that grew naturally in this area for one of our desserts.

I called the Texas A&M extension agency to find out exactly what type of berries they were and whether I could grow them on our property. After a bit of digging, I found that what I thought were dewberries were actually western trailing blackberries. And though they do grow well here, they are spotty in production and not reliable for commercial farming. I wasn't convinced. The extension agent finally gave me the name of a nursery that sold the western trailing blackberry, but the nursery told me the same thing: The berries just wouldn't do well in large production, and for that reason, they refused to sell them to me.

Despite my efforts to use a local berry, we had to settle for frozen blackberries. The cobbler is just as good but without that farm-to-table charm I was hoping to offer.

In making a blackberry cobbler, sometimes the cooking process will cause the berries to disintegrate. When that happens, the end result is blackberry liquid with a cake topping. In order for that not to happen, the berries must remain frozen up until the moment the cobbler is placed into the oven for baking.

For the blackberry filling:
¼ cup sugar
2 tablespoons cornstarch
1 teaspoon vanilla extract
½ tablespoon lemon juice
1 cup of Karo syrup
1 pound blackberries

In a mixing bowl, mix together sugar and cornstarch. In a separate mixing bowl, mix together extract, lemon juice, and Karo syrup. Place blackberries into a 9 x 13–inch baking dish. Combine dry ingredients with blackberries in dish. Mix in wet ingredients until everything is evenly coated. Place blackberry dish into freezer until batter is prepared.

For the batter:
1 cup flour
1 cup sugar
1 tablespoon baking powder
1 egg
2 ounces evaporated milk
6 ounces water
3 ounces butter, melted

Preheat oven to 375 degrees. In mixing bowl, mix first 3 ingredients. In separate bowl, whisk together egg, evaporated milk, and water. Add wet ingredients to dry, mix to form a batter, and then whisk in melted butter. Remove blackberry mixture from freezer and ladle batter on top. Bake for 15 minutes. Reduce heat to 350 degrees, and bake 55 to 60 minutes more, until done.

We began serving blackberry cobbler because it was the closest we could get to Roxie's recipe for dewberry cobbler.

SALT LICK PECAN PIE

THE SALT LICK pecan pie recipe was developed by my dad, Thurman. Not only does it incorporate all of the traditional ingredients that are in a Southern pecan pie, but it also includes a new ingredient: butterscotch. The pecan halves should always be slightly toasted prior to baking in the pie. The toasting enhances the flavor and improves the bite.

For for dough:
1 cup of flour
½ teaspoon of salt
2 tablespoons cold butter
⅓ cup and 1 tablespoon lard
Cold water as needed

Mix together flour and salt. Cut in butter and lard, and mix with a fork until dough starts to clump. Sprinkle with cold water, 1 tablespoon at a time, tossing with fork until all flour is moistened and pastry almost leaves side of bowl. Gather pastry into ball. Shape into flattened round on lightly floured surface. Wrap in plastic and refrigerate about 45 minutes or until dough is firm and cold yet pliable. Slightly firm dough makes pastry flakier. If refrigerated longer, let pastry soften slightly before rolling.

Roll out dough, using floured rolling pin, to ⅛-inch thickness, having it extend 2 inches wider than pie shell. Fold into fourths; place in pie shell. Unfold and ease into shell, pressing firmly against bottom and side. Trim overhanging dough, and fold pastry under, even with plate; crimp the edges.

For for filling:
6 ounces butterscotch pudding mix
¼ cup cornstarch
1 cup sugar
½ cup evaporated milk
3 eggs
1 tablespoon molasses
1 cup Karo syrup
½ teaspoon vanilla extract
½ teaspoon almond extract
1¼ cups lightly toasted pecans

Preheat oven to 375 degrees. Combine pudding mix, cornstarch, and sugar in bowl. In another bowl, mix evaporated milk and eggs. Add molasses, syrup, and extracts, and mix together. Add wet ingredients to dry, and mix until smooth. Place pecans into a pie shell. Add mixture over the pecans, ensuring that all are completely covered. Do not, however, allow any of mixture to spill onto piecrust. Bake 20 minutes; reduce heat to 340, and bake for 70 minutes more, until done.

3,000

PECAN PIE HOW-TO:
[1] Set out all of the necessary ingredients. Preheat oven to 375 degrees.
[2] Combine evaporated milk and eggs in a bowl.

[3-6] Add molasses, syrup, and extracts, and mix together.
[7] Combine pudding mix, cornstarch, and sugar in a bowl.
[8-10] Add wet ingredients to dry, and mix until smooth.
[11-12] Set out pie crust and make sure the edges are pinched evenly.

[13-14] Take a handful of pecans and gently press them into the bottom of the crust to ensure they stay at the bottom while baking.
[15] Add remaining pecans.
[16-18] Slowly pour the pecan pie filling into the piecrust, making sure the pecans are completely covered. [19] Be sure the mixture does not touch the crust edges.
[20] Place in the oven carefully to be sure the mixture does not touch the edges of the crust. Bake according to instructions.
[21] Finished pecan pies from the Salt Lick kitchen.

SUSAN JANELLE GOFF

Susan Janelle Goff

Before John F. Kennedy became president of the United States, he wrote a book titled *Profiles in Courage,* in which he detailed true accounts of eight heroic acts by American patriots in our nation's history. It is an amazing book, and because it speaks about the courageous efforts of Americans, it reminds me to take a moment to think about the people in our own lives who have displayed acts of courage, compassion, and love through difficult times. If you ask me who my personal Profile in Courage is, the answer is Susan Janelle Goff, my wife of 33 years.

After I graduated from college, I treated myself to a vacation on Oahu, Hawaii. My goal for the trip was simply to take full advantage of a leisurely beach lifestyle. I had no idea I would end up meeting my future wife. But there she was on one sunny May afternoon in paradise.

She was living in Hawaii, working on her master's degree in distributive education. She was born in El Paso but had lived in many places throughout her life as the daughter of an Air Force lieutenant colonel. Her last stop before going to college was Austin, where she attended Reagan High School. But her father also had temporary duty in Hawaii when the family was stationed for a while in Omaha. Susan was never able to go with him, but she had always wanted to. She decided to complete her studies there. She moved to Oahu with only $35 in cash and a check for $250 that wouldn't clear until 30 days after she established an address. She had no job and no place to live, but she knew she could make it work.

Susan ended up renting a room from seven sailors who were on duty most of the time. She promised to cook for them and keep house in exchange for rent. She eventually juggled her time between school and four jobs while eating hot dogs and rice to keep costs low. Sometimes, when she couldn't take it anymore, she'd get all dressed up and go down to a bar in hopes a gentleman would buy her a drink. (She once described it to me: "A girl's gotta do what a girl's gotta do.")

When I met her, she had already established a rhythm for herself and made it look so easy to live on the islands. We immediately became inseparable. After I left, we stayed in touch, talking on the phone all the time and promising to visit each other again. Within a few months, she came to visit me in Texas. One night while we were having dinner, she looked at me and asked, "Are you ever going to marry me?" Within a few days we drove down to Wimberley to get our blood tests (a Texas state requirement at the time), and then we went up to Austin and got married at the courthouse. It was only six months from the time we first met on Waikiki.

We didn't tell anyone, because she still had to finish her education in Hawaii and she didn't want her parents to get upset. After she finished school, she came back to Austin to be with me, and we began our life together.

But trouble was in the cards for Susan. Since the age of 14, she had experienced a number of seizures. They were caused by an arterial venal mass formation in her brain that, according to every doctor she consulted, was inoperable without putting her in serious danger. In her case, because of the nature of the mass, it wasn't a matter of if she could have a rupture in one of her arteries, but when. She took on the task of finding someone who could help her. She went all over the country and finally found three doctors who would agree to operate. She settled on a doctor in San Francisco, who seemed to be the most capable and confident for a successful outcome.

Susan had to be at Moffitt Hospital for a few days before the operation for testing and monitoring. She stayed in a long wing of beds with other patients. There was one woman next to her for a few days, and they became good friends, encouraging each other and sharing stories from their lives. It kept her spirits up, and when you're facing such difficult odds, family and friends can be the best remedy.

Just before she was to go into surgery, we spent the evening together at the hospital. We had dinner, and before she settled in for the evening, she hopped out of bed and we danced along the long row of beds in the ward. There wasn't any music playing. It was just us. We danced for a little while, and I remember her smiling at me. We thought it might be our last dance.

Susan never showed fear for what she was about to go through. Her strength and positive nature comforted me more than anything else. As the nurses were wheeling her off to prep her for the procedure, I remember her joking with them, saying, "Now y'all be gentle with me."

Her mother and I sat for an eternity in the waiting room before the doctor came in, seven hours later, and told me everything looked great. He said that he had never had an operation go that well but that the procedure wasn't completely finished. The operation required a lot of blood, and he wanted to wait a couple of days for her to stabilize before finishing. He suggested we go home and come back in the morning. Susan's mother refused to leave before we checked on her. So I made my way back to the recovery room, a strange dark room with only Susan and another patient, visible by a single spotlight over their beds. It was so cold in there you could see your breath. Susan was sleeping soundly, and I felt confident that we could go.

At 2 o'clock the next morning, the doctor called, asking us to come back. When we got there, ambulances were storming the hospital from all over. Susan had experienced a rupture from the surgery and was having massive bleeding. The ambulances had to rush all of the blood from the entire Bay Area to help her. That night, the medical team went through 52 units of blood, and when they were finished, only 2 units remained in the Bay Area. They couldn't stop the bleeding. They ended up just giving up. They were able to pack the rupture, and they put Susan in a barbiturate coma.

When the doctor came out to report the progress, he saw my face and he collapsed against the wall in exhaustion. He told me what had happened to her, apologized, and said he had never lost a patient like that. My heart sank. He was telling me that she didn't make it. Despite the horrible odds we were facing for this procedure, I still couldn't imagine my life without Susan. After I was able to collect myself, I asked the doctor what I needed to do to get her body back to Texas for a funeral there.

He said the protocol required him to keep her on a respirator for 72 hours before he could turn it off. She wasn't technically dead, but once the respirator was turned off, she would not be able to breathe on her own. So we waited. For three agonizing days. The doctors showed me pictures of her brain, and I could see that the damage was almost the size of her whole brain. When it came time to discontinue the respirator, though, she kept breathing. Her body continued to function beautifully. After a little while, she began to wake up and the very first thing she did was smile. It was one of the most radiant smiles I've ever seen.

Susan has never fully recovered from that experience, and she has had many other procedures since then to improve her prognosis. She was in a wheelchair for two years before she began to walk again. She had to completely relearn how to communicate. For a long time, the only words she could say were "Ever, ever." I managed to figure out what she was trying to say by the different tone or inflection she used as she repeated those words. Her doctor said that after about two years, her progress would halt, but it's been more than 30 years and she has proved him wrong. She gradually continues to get better every day.

Today Susan still struggles to walk and has limited ability in her arm movement. She has regained some of her vocabulary, and perhaps the biggest miracle of all is that we had a daughter, Maile, just a few years after the surgery. Susie has been a doting and devoted mother to her. My wife is also responsible for the continued success of the Salt Lick. There have been many times I have wanted to close the place down, but she wouldn't let me. She insisted I update the restaurant and kept on me to improve operations, which has turned the Salt Lick into what it is today. In many ways, without her, there might not have been a Salt Lick to visit anymore.

The one thing about Susan is her indomitable spirit. After all of the horrible medical procedures she has endured, including the one that almost took her life, she never lost her spirit to live, and she has never lost her radiant smile.

I'll never forget the time we had return for a check-up with the doctor in San Francisco. It was the first time she had left the house since recovering from that surgery. She was still not able to speak, but we had figured out our own method of communicating. She weighed only about 70 pounds, and her hair had not fully grown back, so she wore a turban. We had finished our doctor's appointment with positive feedback. She wanted to drive around Lombard Street. When we got to the intersection of Lombard and Scott, we found a restaurant called Scott's Seafood Grill and Bar. Because of the name, we decided to stop for dinner. We ordered a few courses and started getting to know our server. We told him why we were in town and about Susan's experience. I think I had some sort of grouper dish, and she ordered a seafood sauté that was just delicious. Susan absolutely loved it. When the server came back to take our dessert order, she kept trying to indicate that she wanted

In 1976 the first Scott's Seafood Grill and Bar opened at the corner of Scott and Lombard in San Francisco, hence the name. The tiny 40-seat restaurant was an immediate success, becoming one of the top 10 restaurants in the United States in volume per seat in just a few months. In 1991 restaurant ownership changed hands to Alan Irvine and John Cook and the restaurant moved to the Sacramento area.

something specific. It took me a while to figure out that she wanted that exact same seafood sauté dish for dessert.

The next thing we knew, the chef came out to talk to us. He wanted to meet the person who had ordered a second helping of his dish. We talked with him for a while, and he was moved by Susan's story. He thanked her for having such a strong spirit and said her meal was on the house. (I'm pretty sure I still had to pay for mine.) Susan's strength and positive attitude is infectious. It's amazing to meet people in life who go through turmoil and struggle yet seem to greet each new day with a smile. Susan is one of those people, and I've been blessed to have her with me every day since we met.

I've included a variation on the seafood sauté from Scott's Seafood Grill and Bar. Though the restaurant opened at the corner of Lombard and Scott in 1976 and was one of the top 10 restaurants in the country, it changed hands in 1991 into a split ownership. One Scott's in Oakland serves much of the same menu, and another Scott's is under the ownership of Alan Irvine, who began his career as an assistant manager at the original Lombard Street restaurant. He has since moved the restaurant to Sacramento, with three separate locations. Alan was generous enough to give us this recipe variation.

This recipe is dedicated to my personal Profile in Courage, Susan Janelle Goff. She has always been, and forever will be, my inspiration. This dish is best served for a special occasion and for someone who can greet each new challenge in life with strength and a radiant smile.

SCOTT'S SEAFOOD GRILL AND BAR SEAFOOD SAUTÉ

For the velouté:
¼ pound sweet butter
½ cup flour
1 pint whole milk
¾ cup fish stock
1 bay leaf
Salt and white pepper to taste

For the lemon-butter sauce:
½ cup sherry
½ cup fish stock
1 teaspoon chopped fresh garlic
1 teaspoon chopped fresh shallots
½ cup velouté
1½ tablespoons lemon juice
1¼ cup sweet butter
1 teaspoon salt
White pepper to taste

For each serving:

1 ounce olive oil

3 16/20 Mexican white prawns, cleaned and peeled

2 U-10 scallops, boots removed

2 dungeness fry legs

Kosher salt and fresh ground black pepper

1 teaspoon chopped fresh shallots

1 teaspoon chopped fresh garlic

2 ounces white wine

1 tablespoon fresh lemon juice

3 ounces lemon butter sauce (see recipe)

For the velouté: melt butter over medium heat in a heavy saucepan. Add flour and cook until roux is smooth. Heat milk, stock, and bay leaves to scalding point. Slowly add roux to milk mixture with bur mixer. Reduce heat and cook for one hour, stirring frequently. Season to taste. Makes approximately 2 pints.

For the lemon-butter sauce: reduce sherry, stock, garlic, and shallots by half. Add velouté and mix together until smooth. Add lemon juice and reduce heat. Add butter, whisking slowly until incorporated. Add salt and pepper. Strain through fine mesh cap. Makes 2 ½ cups.

For the seafood sauté: heat olive oil in sauté pan over medium-high heat. Add prawns, scallops, and crab. Season well with salt and pepper. When prawns start to turn red and scallops have a nice crust, turn shellfish over and add shallots and garlic. Sauté for 1 more minute to soften shallots and garlic. Deglaze pan with white wine and lemon juice. Reduce until almost no liquid is left. Add lemon butter, immediately remove from heat, and toss. Serve with white rice, rice pilaf, or fettucine.

Susan has improved so much over the years that on my 50th birthday she was able to dance again. It turns out she's a much better dancer than me.

BEYOND THE SALT LICK

★ ★ ★

AFTER I BEGAN running the restaurant, in the late eighties, I increasingly began to get requests to cater events. And in addition to our usual barbecue fare, people started asking for other options. For us it was a great opportunity to expand on what we could do and gave us the chance to be creative.

People were always begging us to bring our food to their weddings, office parties, and home events. We added a large commissary to the main restaurant building to give us more space for larger events. That also gave us an opportunity to accommodate larger parties that couldn't fit in the dining rooms. One year we even had a request from movie producer Jerry Bruckheimer to fly out to his ranch in California for his 50th birthday. That's probably the farthest we've gone to cater an event—but it was worth it.

The barbecue itself has gone further than that. We started the mail-order side of the business in 1996 as a result of Ben Crenshaw's winning the Masters Tournament the year before. When you win the Masters, you get to go back to Georgia and host a "past champions" dinner. The only guys in the room are the guys in the special Masters green jackets. Crenshaw called and asked if I would serve Salt Lick barbecue for the dinner he was hosting. But we couldn't enter to cater, so I figured out a way to freeze the food and still keep its flavor. And we sent it off to Georgia. After that we began offering it as a service, to ship barbecue all over the country.

The farthest we've shipped in the U.S. is to Hawaii. I later learned the farthest we've ever shipped it: I got a call from Fort Hood for an order and found out the food was then shipped to a soldier serving in Iraq. Had I known it was going there, I would have shipped more.

A few years ago we started promoting online sales for barbecue. It stays pretty steady throughout the year, but during the holidays it just gets kind of crazy. We've had the UPS truck backed up to load its entire bed with barbecue to ship.

A FRIEND OF MINE wanted us to cater her wedding a few years back. She requested our barbecue for her main dinner but wanted a passed appetizer to serve to guests during the beginning of her reception. When I asked her what she wanted, she just said, "A barbecued appetizer, of course." I didn't exactly know how to conceptualize that at first, considering nothing that we serve is exactly dainty finger food. She told me to use my imagination and "dream it up" for her. After many nights, I didn't have a single dream with a good idea, but I finally settled on a twist on stuffed mushrooms, an appetizer people always seem to love. This is what we came up with.

BRISKET-STUFFED MUSHROOMS

2 chopped briskets (half loin, half deckle)
1 cup cheddar cheese, grated
1 bunch green onions, chopped
½ cup Panko bread crumbs
4 ounces Salt Lick Lauren's Spicy Recipe Bar-B-Que Sauce
Salt and pepper to taste
30 large white mushrooms, stemmed
1 bunch flat leaf parsley for garnish, chopped

Preheat oven to 350 degrees. Combine first 6 ingredients in large bowl and stuff spoonful of mixture into each mushroom cap. Place 12 mushroom caps on baking sheet, and top each with small dollop of Lauren's Spicy Recipe sauce. Bake 10 to 15 minutes, or until golden brown on top. Continue with remaining caps. Garnish with chopped parsley, and serve.

BRISKET JALAPEÑO POPPERS

THE IDEA for brisket poppers came to me while sitting at an airport bar, waiting for a flight to Cozumel. My friends and I split an order of jalepeño poppers and brisket. To wash it down, some ice-cold beer. Then the thought came to me: smoked brisket, jalapeños, cheese—these should all be married together and fried to a golden crunchiness. We've since served these at countless events. It just goes to show you never to discount great inspirations while sitting at an airport bar.

Peanut or canola oil for frying
½ pound chopped brisket
1 egg, whisked
4 ounces diced pickled jalapeño
½ tablespoon Salt Lick Garlic Dry Rub mix
6 tablespoons Salt Lick Bar-B-Que Sauce
½ cup Panko breadcrumbs
3 ounces American cheese, shredded
3 ounces Swiss cheese, grated

Heat oil in deep fryer to 350 degrees. In large mixing bowl, combine brisket and egg and mix well. Add jalapeño, dry rub mix, and barbecue sauce, and mix well. Add breadcrumbs in small amounts and make sure they are evenly distributed. Add cheeses, and mix well. Scoop ½-ounce spoonfuls of mix to form poppers. Fry in oil until golden brown. Remove and drain on paper towel. Yields about 20 poppers.

BRISKET BURRITOS

I LOVE flour tortillas—especially when they're fresh. I love barbecue brisket—especially the way we do it. And I love burritos—especially when it combines those two ingredients. You can add whatever else you like, but even if you don't, this is the best way to enjoy barbecue in a perfect little package.

4 ounces fresh chopped beef brisket
1 ounces Salt Lick Bar-B-Que Sauce
2 ounces chopped onion
1 ounces chopped tomato
2 ounces beans
2 ounces shredded cheddar cheese
1 10-inch flour tortilla, warmed

Layer ingredients off-center on tortilla. Fold sides and ends over filling, and roll up. Serves 1.

Putting a Salt Lick barbecue twist on classic Texas dishes has been one of the most rewarding parts about catering events. People still love the barbecue flavor. It's just delivered in a slightly different package.

TEXAS CHIMICHANGA

FOR OUR VERSION of a Texified chimichanga, pan fry burrito in hot canola oil until crisp on both sides, and serve with cheese sauce from the Brisket Burger (recipe on page 268) and our Chili con Carne (below).

CHILI CON CARNE

I'VE EATEN chili con carne in a variety of different ways throughout my life. It's an essential Texas dish. I think this old recipe gives the best interpretation of what the Texas early immigrants were trying to accomplish—accentuating the rich taste of meat and the chile itself.

2 to 3 pounds cubed beef
White pepper to taste
2 teaspoons lard or bacon grease, more as needed
1 chopped onion
2 cups beef stock
1 tablespoon chili powder
1 teaspoon cumin
1 teaspooon oregano
⅛ to ¼ teaspoon cayenne
1 teaspoon sugar
¼ cup tomato paste

Coat beef with white pepper and pan fry in lard or grease until browned. Place on paper towels to drain. Heat grease in cast-iron skillet, and sauté onions until translucent. In large saucepan, cast-iron skillet, or Dutch oven, place meat, pan juices, and onions. Add beef stock and remaining ingredients, and stir well. Simmer uncovered for 1¾ hours, or until beef is tender. If mixture dries out or thickens too much, add more stock.

NOTE: No beans. Tomato paste can be left out. If you are a sissy, substitute vegetable oil for bacon grease or lard. If flavor is lacking, add a little garlic powder.

SMOKED BRISKET BURGER

IT SEEMS everyone has their own take on the classic hamburger. We, of course, had to add some of our brisket to the mix. You don't have to use the cheese sauce if you don't want things to get too messy, but if you're going to be eating with your hands anyway, why not make the best of it?

Roasted peppers:
1 of each bell pepper (gold, red, green)
½ red onion

Preheat oven to 375 degrees. Slice and combine peppers. Place on baking sheet and lightly drizzle olive oil. Roast in oven until medium roasted. Set aside in container. Slice raw red onion, and add to peppers.

Cheese sauce:
2½ pounds extra melt cheese (Velveeta is fine)
½ quart half-and-half

Cut cheese into small chunks and place in saucepan over medium low heat or in a slow cooker. Be careful not to scorch. Add half-and-half when cheese is melted, and stir well.

Smoked burger:
5 pounds ground beef (80/20)
3 pounds lean chopped brisket
6 ounces Salt Lick Lauren's Spicy Recipe Bar-B-Que Sauce
1 tablespoon salt
1 tablespoon pepper
1 dozen buns, toasted

Combine ground beef and chopped brisket in large mixing bowl. Add barbecue sauce, salt, and pepper. Form into 12 burgers and grill on a hot grill for 5 to 7 minutes on each side, depending on your preference for doneness. Remove from heat, and let rest for 5 minutes. Serve on buns with roasted peppers and cheese sauce.

VENISON BLACK BEAN CHILI

THE OLD FOLKS mostly fried their venison. The rest of the venison was usually made into breakfast sausage. What little venison chili I remember never had black beans. As a matter of fact, except for this recipe, you should never add beans to chili. Since this chili is not beef chili, though, I guess we can let it go, but just this once.

2 tablespoons bacon grease
2 pounds venison shoulder, cut into ½-inch pieces
Salt and pepper
1 large red onion, finely diced
3 cloves garlic, minced
½ pound smoked sausage, chopped
3 cups chicken stock
1 cup chopped plum tomatoes (2 medium)
2 tablespoons tomato paste
½ teaspoon chipotle pepper pureé
2 tablespoons ancho chile powder
2 teaspoons pasilla chile powder
1½ teaspoons honey
1 8-ounce can black beans, drained
1 tablespoon lime juice

In large Dutch oven over high heat, heat grease. Season venison with salt and pepper, and saute until browned. Remove meat and all but 3 tablespoons of fat. Reduce heat to medium. Saute onions until translucent. Add garlic, and cook 2 minutes. Return venison to pot, add sausage, chicken stock, tomatoes and tomato paste, chipotle pureé, chile powders, and honey. Increase heat until mixture boils, then cover and simmer about 45 minutes. Add beans, and cook an additional 15 minutes. Remove from heat, and add lime juice. Taste to see if any additions are needed.

Toppings:
Fried corn tortilla strips
Mexican cotija cheese or goat cheese
Fresh cilantro leaves

To serve, ladle chili into warm bowls. Top with cheese, then top with tortilla strips. Sprinkle cilantro on top. This is another dish that goes well with jalapeño cornbread. If the chili is too spicy for you, leave jalapeño out of the cornbread (recipe on page 159).

SMOKED PULLED PORK MUSHROOM STEW

In the spring of 2002, Jay Knepp and I planted our first vineyard. We planted Sangiovese and Tempranillo in soil that according to analysis was better that 99 percent of the soil in California for growing grapes. Neither of us had any experience in growing grapes. By some miracle, when October rolled around, 99 percent of them were alive and flourishing. So we invited 150 of our best friends and neighbors to celebrate. Now we are about to have our 10th annual celebration.

We served this recipe at the first vineyard dinner.

⅓ cup all-purpose flour
2 teaspoons Italian herb seasoning
½ teaspoon salt
½ teaspoon pepper
3 pounds boneless shoulder butt pork roasts, trimmed and cut into 1-inch cubes
3 tablespoons vegetable oil
2 onions, chopped
4 garlic cloves, minced
2 cups peeled pearl onions
2 cups beef or chicken stock
1 bay leaf
4 cups trimmed oyster mushrooms or button mushrooms
½ cup frozen peas

This is our idea of a good old Southern comfort dish. It's flavorful and filling, and it tastes even better the next day for leftovers.

Preheat oven to 350 degrees. In large bowl, whisk together flour and half each of the Italian herb seasoning, salt, and pepper. Add pork in batches, and toss to coat. Reserve leftover flour mixture. In large Dutch oven, heat oil over medium high heat; brown pork in batches. Transfer to plate. Drain fat from pan, and reduce heat to medium. Cook onions, garlic, and remaining Italian herb seasoning, salt, and pepper, stirring occasionally, until onions are softened, about 5 minutes.

Stir in pearl onions and reserved flour mixture, and cook, stirring occasionally, for 5 minutes. Add stock and bay leaf. Bring to boil, scraping up brown bits from bottom of pan. Return pork and accumulated juices to pan. Cover and cook in oven until pork is tender, about 1 hour. Stir in mushrooms and peas. Cook, uncovered, until mushrooms are tender and sauce is slightly thickened, about 15 minutes. Discard bay leaf.

Cheesy polenta:

5 cups water

1 teaspoon salt

1¼ cups uncooked quick-cooking grits

1 cup shredded sharp cheddar cheese

1 cup shredded asagio cheese

½ cup heavy cream

2 tablespoons butter

¼ teaspoon white pepper

Bring water and salt to a boil in medium saucepan over medium high heat. Gradually whisk in grits, and bring back to a boil. Reduce heat to medium low and simmer, stirring occasionally, 10 minutes or until thickened. Stir in remaining ingredients until cheese is melted and mixture is blended. Serve immediately.

Stone-ground grits may be substituted. Increase water to 6 cups and increase cook time to 50 minutes. *NOTE: For testing purposes only, we used White Lily Quick Grits.*

In large pot, add pulled pork and mushrooms over medium heat while stirring. Bring to serving temperature, and serve with cheesy polenta.

SMOKED TURKEY ENCHILADAS

SMOKED TURKEY ENCHILADAS

THIS IS A RECIPE I worked up one year for leftovers from Thanksgiving turkey. Now I look forward to it more than the actual Thanksgiving meal.

Sour cream gravy:
2 tomatillos
3 teaspoons butter
2 cloves garlic, minced
3 teaspoons flour
¼ teaspoon cayenne pepper
¼ teaspoon pepper
3 teaspoons salt, or to taste
1 cup chicken broth
2 cups sour cream

Filling:
6 tablespoons butter
2 teaspoons minced garlic
¼ cup minced onion
8 ounces white mushrooms, chopped, stems included
16 ounces smoked turkey, shredded and chopped
1 teaspoon chili dulce
½ teaspoon white pepper
Salt to taste

Assembly:
3 tablespoons oil
12 corn tortillas
1 cup shredded asiago cheese
1 cup American cheddar

All around the Salt Lick we've got little reminders of where we're from. Whether it's an old boot filled with fresh wildflowers or the framed Texas flag in one of our dining rooms, we want everyone to remember that their best barbecue experience is in Texas.

For sour cream gravy: Cut tomatillos in quarters and place in a hot cast-iron skillet, caramelize and char the edges, turn, and repeat. Peel the skins from the tomatillos. Place in a food processor and pureé. Cool and reserve. Melt butter in cast-iron skill over medium heat, add garlic, and sauté until translucent. Add flour, cayenne, white pepper, and salt, and stir to make a white roux. Add chicken broth, and cook about 1 minute, until you have gravy. Add the tomatillo puree. Remove from pan and allow to cool to room temperature. Place sour cream in large bowl, and gently spoon in gravy. Stir until mixed, and refrigerate.

For filling: Place butter in saucepan over low heat and melt. Add garlic, onion, and mushrooms. Cook slowly until mushrooms are tender, keeping them from turning dark. Add turkey. Stir in chili dulce and white pepper, and season with salt to taste.

For assembly: Preheat oven to 325 degrees. Heat a little oil in skillet over medium heat. Cook tortillas on each side about 2 minutes or until soft. Replenish oil as

necessary. Wrap in cloth to keep warm as you cook all 12. Cover bottom of casserole with sour cream gravy. (Do not use all of it, but reserve some for later.) Place on each tortilla ⅓ cup turkey filling and 1 tablespoon of each cheese. Roll tortillas around filling and place seam-side down in casserole dish. Cover enchiladas with remaining gravy and sprinkle remaining cheese on top. Bake for 25 minutes, or until top is brown and bubbling. Serves 6 to 8.

SMOKED BRISKET YUCCA HASH WITH SOUTHERN BASTED EGG

WHAT DO YOU DO with leftover smoked brisket? Tacos, burritos, brisket poppers, brisket burger, chili con carne, and Texas chimichangas come to mind. For breakfast, though, brisket in cream gravy over biscuits and this recipe come to mind.

2 pounds yucca
Kosher salt to taste
½ cup canola oil
1 cup chopped shishito peppers or green bell peppers
2 cloves garlic, minced
1 onion, sliced
Pepper to taste
2 teaspoons paprika
Butter or bacon grease
8 to 10 eggs

Peel yucca and cut into 1-inch cubes. Place in a large pot of salted water and bring to a boil. Simmer and cook until tender, about 15 minutes. Drain and allow to cool. Set a large skillet over medium-high heat. Add oil and fry yucca until crispy, 10 to 12 minutes. Transfer to a paper towel–lined plate to drain, and season with salt. Add peppers and onions to pan, and sauté until onions are transluscent. Fold the crispy yucca back into the pan, and heat through. Season with salt, pepper, and paprika.

Cover the bottom of a small skillet that barely holds one egg with butter or bacon grease, place on medium heat until grease is hot, and add egg. Let egg set, add 2 tablespoons water, cover, and cook to desired doneness. Plate yucca hash, and add cooked egg on top. Repeat to cook the remaining eggs. Serves 8 to 10.

Yucca is a potato-like root vegetable commonly found in South America. You can find it in the produce department of your local grocery store.

❧ MARDI GRAS MENU ❧

THERE WAS a time when I lived in Tupelo, Miss. I did a little spin-off from the Salt Lick and took the opportunity to diverge from the standard barbecue my parents had served while I was growing up. As a nod to Southern-style Cajun cooking, I made a special Mardi Gras menu. We served a combination platter with shrimp Creole, crawfish étouffée, and red beans and rice, with a bread pudding dessert, for $9.95.

SHRIMP CREOLE

12 medium-size firm ripe tomatoes
     or 4 cups coarsely chopped drained canned tomatoes
3 pounds uncooked medium shrimp (20 to 24 per pound)
½ cup vegetable oil
2 cups coarsely chopped onions
1 cup coarsely chopped green peppers
1 cup coarsely chopped celery
2 teaspoons finely chopped garlic
1 cup water
2 medium bay leaves
1 tablespoon paprika
½ teaspoon ground cayenne pepper
1 tablespoon salt
2 tablespoons cornstarch mixed with ¼ cup cold water
Butter to taste
6 to 8 cups freshly cooked long-grain white rice

If using fresh tomatoes, drop 3 or 4 at a time into pan of boiling water and remove after 15 seconds. Run cold water over them and peel with small sharp knife. Cut out stems, then slice in half crosswise and squeeze gently to remove seeds and juice. Chop coarsely.

Shell shrimp. Devein by making shallow incision down back with small sharp knife and lifting out black or white intestinal vein with point of knife. Wash shrimp in colander under cold running water, and spread on paper towels to drain.

In heavy 4- to 5-quart casserole, heat the oil over moderate heat until light haze forms above it. Add onions, peppers, celery, and garlic, and stirring frequently, cook for about 5 minutes, or until vegetables are soft and translucent but not brown. Stir in tomatoes, water, bay leaves, paprika, cayenne, and salt, and bring to boil over high heat. Reduce the heat to low, cover casserole partially, and stirring occasionally, simmer mixture 20 to 25 minutes, or until thick enough to hold its shape almost solidly in spoon. Stir in shrimp and continue to simmer, partially covered, for about 5 minutes longer, or until they are pink and firm to the touch.

Stir cornstarch and water mixture once or twice to recombine, and pour into casserole. Stir over low heat for 2 to 3 minutes, until sauce thickens slightly. Pick out and discard bay leaves, taste sauce for seasoning, add butter, and let it melt in.

Serve Shrimp Creole at once, directly from the casserole, accompanied by rice in a separate bowl. Or, if you prefer, mound rice on a deep-heated platter and ladle Shrimp Creole around it.

CRAWFISH ÉTOUFFÉE

ÉTOUFFÉE MEANS "smothered," and in this dish the crawfish tails are blackened with a rich, thick sauce.

2 cups fish stock
4 tablespoons brown roux
1 cup finely chopped onions
1 cup finely chopped scallions, including 3 inches of green tops
½ cup finely chopped celery
1 teaspoon finely chopped garlic
1-pound can tomatoes, drained and finely chopped
1 tablespoon Worcestershire sauce
¼ teaspoon ground cayenne pepper
1 teaspoon freshly ground black pepper
2 teaspoons salt
2½ pounds large crawfish tails
4 to 6 cups freshly cooked baked rice (see Red Beans and Rice Sauté)

Bring fish stock to a boil in small saucepan over high heat. Remove pan from heat and cover to keep hot. In heavy 5- to 6-quart casserole, warm brown roux over low heat for 2 or 3 minutes, stirring constantly. Add onions, scallions, celery, and garlic, and stirring frequently, cook over moderate heat for about 5 minutes, or until vegetables are soft. Then, stirring constantly, pour in hot fish stock in slow, thin stream, and cook over high heat until mixture comes to a boil and thickens lightly.

Add tomatoes, Worcestershire, cayenne, black pepper, and salt, and reduce heat to low. Simmer partially covered for 30 minutes, then stir in crawfish meat and heat through. Taste for seasoning, and ladle étouffée into heated bowl. Mound rice in a separate bowl, and serve at once. Serves 4.

RED BEANS AND RICE

6 cups water
1 pound dried small red beans or dried kidney beans
4 tablespoons butter
½ cup finely chopped onions
1 teaspoon finely chopped garlic
1 cup finely chopped scallions, including 3 inches of green tops
2 1-pound smoked ham hocks
1 teaspoon salt, or more to taste
1 teaspoon freshly ground black pepper
½ pound smoked sausage, chopped
6 to 8 cups baked rice (recipe on page below)

In heavy 3- to 4-quart saucepan, bring water to a boil over high heat. Drop in beans and boil briskly, uncovered, for 2 minutes. Then turn off heat, and let the beans soak for 1 hour. Drain in sieve over large bowl; measure soaking liquid and, if necessary, add more water to make 4 cups. Set beans and liquid aside.

Melt butter in heavy 4- to 5-quart Dutch oven set over moderate heat. When foam begins to subside, add onions, garlic, and ½ of scallions, and stirring frequently, cook for about 5 minutes, or until soft and translucent but not brown.

Stir in beans and liquid, ham hocks, salt, and pepper. Bring mixture to a boil over high heat, reduce heat to low, and simmer, partially covered, for about 3 hours, or until beans are very soft. Check pot from time to time, and if beans seem dry, add up to 1 cup more water, a few tablespoons at a time. During last 30 minutes or so of cooking, stir frequently and mash softest beans against sides of pan to form thick sauce for remaining beans.

With tongs or a slotted spoon, transfer the ham hocks to a plate. Cut the meat away from the bones and remove and discard the skin fat and gristle. Cut the meat into ¼ inch dice and return it to the beans. Taste beans for seasoning, and serve with smoked sausage. Plate baked rice, ladle red beans over rice, and sprinkle on remaining chopped scallion. Serves 6.

OVEN BAKED RICE

6 cups rice
10 cups chicken broth
6 tablespoons finely chopped celery
6 tablespoons finely chopped onion
6 tablespoons finely chopped green pepper
½ teaspoon granulated garlic
Dash cayenne
Pinch white pepper
6 tablespoons butter

A lot of people don't realize just how easy it can be to make a perfect batch of rice in the oven rather than on the stove top. This recipe has always yielded perfect rice every time.

Preheat oven to 350 degrees. Mix all ingredients except butter in long shallow pan. Add butter evenly over ingredients in pan. Cover tightly in aluminum foil. Bake for approximately 1 hour.

BREAD PUDDING

2 tablespoons butter, softened
12 ounces day-old French or Italian white bread
1 quart milk
3 eggs
2 cups sugar
½ cup seedless raisins
2 tablespoons vanilla extract

Sauce ingredients:
8 tablespoons butter, cut into ½-inch chunks
1 cup sugar
1 egg
½ cup bourbon

Preheat oven to 350 degrees. With pastry brush, spread softened butter evenly over bottom and sides of 13 x 9 baking dish. Set aside. Break bread into chunks, dropping it into large bowl, and pour milk over it. When bread is softened, crumble into small bits and let it continue to soak until all milk is absorbed.

In small bowl, beat eggs and sugar together. Stir in raisins and vanilla. Pour egg mixture over bread, and stir until all ingredients are well combined. Pour bread pudding into buttered dish, spreading it evenly and smoothing top with rubber spatula. Place dish in large shallow roasting pan set on middle shelf of oven, and pour boiling water into pan to depth of about 1 inch. Bake 1 hour, or until a knife inserted in center of pudding comes out clean.

For the sauce: Melt butter bits in double boiler over hot but not boiling water. In separate bowl, stir together sugar and egg, then slowly add mixture to melted butter. Stir until sugar dissolves, 2 to 3 minutes. The egg will cook, but do not let sauce come to a boil or egg will curdle. Remove pan from heat, and let sauce cool to room temperature before stirring in bourbon. Serve bread pudding from the oven immediately, with warm bourbon sauce on top.

A NOTE ON THE WHISKEY SAUCE FOR THE BREAD PUDDING: You'll notice we don't flare the alcohol out of the sauce, so you may want to be careful when you serve it. We once served it to a party of 75 senior citizens on a tour boat down the Mississippi River. The boat captain later told me, "Whatever you do, don't change the bread pudding recipe. Normally senior citizens are a grumpy lot, but this was the most enjoyable trip I've ever taken."

❧ SALT LICK VINEYARDS ❧

OUR NEWEST ENDEAVOR is the Salt Lick Cellars. I had always wanted to find something that we could grow here that would reflect my family's history in farming and local agriculture. But I wasn't going to even mess with cotton. One year I tried to establish an orchard of peaches. I planted 850 trees, but they failed miserably. I later found out that I would need to plant what really does well in the Driftwood soil, which is grapes. I adore wine. And the Texas wine industry has grown by leaps and bounds in the past 10 years. So I decided to plant a vineyard. A small one, with only 3 acres (I may consider olives later down the line).

I asked a friend of mine, Jay Knepp, who used to manage Mezzaluna, a restaurant in Austin that my wife and I loved to frequent, if he would be interested in helping me out. He said yes, and the rest was, well, a long process of testing soils, selecting root stocks, ordering vines, and actually getting them in the ground. You have to wait a year or so before you can even get good grapes. But that time, the soil was in our favor. We sent samples of the soil to Texas A&M University as well as to the Seghesio Family Vineyards in Alexander Valley, Calif., which helped to mentor Jay when he was younger. The folks there told Jay, "Do you know what you have here? According to the samples you sent, the dirt you have is better than 99 percent of the soil in California. People in California have worked for more than 30 years to get their soil this good, and it's still not there. They would kill to get this kind of dirt." Then they said, "But, of course, you don't have our California climate."

Onion Creek has been the saving grace in our endeavor to plant a vineyard. The deposits of various soils it has brought to this valley over the years has made it one of the prime spots in Texas to grow grapes.

I have to thank Onion Creek for giving us such great soil. The creek meanders dramatically throughout our property, and as a result, the soil that has been deposited over the years through floods and decomposition has been a boon for our vineyard endeavor. We later learned that the average dirt on a Hill Country ranch is about 2.5 inches deep before you hit limestone. We average 3 to 5 feet. In some places, we have been able to dig 16 to 18 feet without running into rock. It'a all due to the deposits from Onion Creek. The more we researched, the more we realized we were on the right track with grapes. When my family settled here more than 100 years ago, they raised cotton. My grandparents and parents farmed vegetables and small yield crops. Today, we're continuing our family's agricultural heritage, but with vineyards.

The Seghesios were right. We don't have the same climate as California. But we do have a climate similar to Spain, Southern France, and Italy. If there's anything I've learned from the many pioneers of the Texas wine industry who have progressed through trial and error, it is that the Texas Hill Country is best suited for warm-climate grapes. If we keep our eyes focused on the grapes that do well in warm regions, we're on the right track. Just above the Salt Lick, on a sloping hillside, we planted 2 acres of Tempranillo grapes. At four years, the vines were performing as if it had been eight years.

I looked to my friends, Ed and Susan Auler of Fall Creek Vineyards, to make a wine from the Tempranillo grapes I planted. The Aulers are some of the pioneers of the Texas wine industry, making wine in the state since the mid-1970s. In 2008 they released their first production of Tempranillo, with 250 cases. It had availability only in restaurants because of its low production, but the reception was unbelievable.

With that bit of confidence, we expanded our vineyards and doubled our acreage in grapes to 5 total acres, adding the Italian Sangiovese grape. Then, in true Texas fashion, we went crazy and planted 30 more acres the following year, expanding our grape varietals to include Mourvedre, Syrah, and Grenache. As of 2011, we have a total of 35 acres planted, with plans to expand to 65 to 70 acres by 2013.

While we used the Tempranillo as a test crop and our partnership with the Aulers still remains, I wanted to move on to the next step with the vineyards and sell wine under our own label. In 2010 we unveiled the Salt Lick Cellars. Jay manages our wine operations, and my daughter, Maile, will run the business and marketing side of the Cellars (with a lot of that same "wisdom" from me that I received from my mom when I first started running the restaurant). We have partnered with Hill Country winemakers from Fall Creek Vineyards, Duchman Family Winery, McPherson Cellars, and William Chris Winery to make wines using our grapes that we now sell under our own label.

The first releases under the Salt Lick Cellars label included two special blends to pair specifically with our barbecue, a BBQ Red, made predominantly of Zinfandel, and a BBQ White, made with albarino. Since then, we have also released a Syrah, a Tempranillo, a Mourvedre, and a Sangiovese, which won *Texas Monthly* magazine's Texas Wine of the Month.

Jay Knepp – Wine Operations

IF YOU HAD told me 20 years ago I would be managing a winery and vineyard, I wouldn't have believed you. Although I fell in love with the production of wine at an early age, I didn't think I'd have an opportunity to do it for a living. I grew up in Northern California and went to school in Santa Barbara, near the St. Ynez Valley. My uncle was a cotton farmer in the Bakersfield area, and when I was a young teenager, I spent a lot of time going up to his farm and learning the ropes as a farmer. I loved the farming life. I loved just looking down row after row of cotton.

When I was older, I saw the vineyards in Napa for the first time, and I was in love again. I put myself through college in the restaurant business and ended up staying in that business. While I was in school, I went up for weekends to the wine country. I wasn't even old enough to drink, but I signed up for winery tours just so I could see how it was all done. Sometimes the wineries wouldn't let me go, but most of them would let me come along to learn.

While running a restaurant in California, I met my wife, Charlotte, a native Texan. After we had been dating a few years, she wanted to move back home to Texas. Although I really liked her at the time, I wasn't quite ready to move to Texas. I had grown up in Marin County, had gone to high school in Carmel, and had lived in Aspen for a few years. Texas wasn't really on my radar for laying down roots. But I had never been to the Hill Country. Once I saw it, I realized what I was missing. It also didn't hurt that real estate was so much more affordable in Texas than in California. So I eventually caved and came to Texas to be with her.

We got married and worked into the restaurant scene of Austin. When Mezzaluna opened up downtown in 1990, I got a job managing both the restaurant and the wine program for nine years. It was an amazing restaurant, with a dedication to wine. We had an award-winning wine list and incentive programs for staff to know wine. My employer would send me to California and Italy to learn more about wine tasting and production. It was a full-time job just to manage the business, but I learned the most about wine during my time there.

That's when I met Scott Roberts and Susan Goff. They were regulars at the bar, and we even had two seats set up at the end of the bar for them whenever they showed up. We always talked about wine, and it was wine that brought us together as great friends. A few years later, Scott asked me if I'd help him with a vineyard out on the Salt Lick property. Somehow I felt like my whole life had prepared me to do it: I had grown up around farming and wine grapes. I immediately accepted.

APPLE-JICAMA CHIPOTLE SLAW

IN 2011 WE WERE invited to New York to the 26th Annual Chef's Tribute to honor James Beard and benefit Citymeals-on-Wheels. We were among a number of well-known American chefs, including Daniel Bouloud, Tom Colicchio, Jean-George Vong-erichten, Jonathan Waxman, and Nobu Matsuhisa. They wanted us to serve up a taste of home, which meant that we would, of course, serve barbecue. Of the some 40 booths that were set up in Rockefeller Center, ours was the only one that had a continuous line that wrapped around the block. We even had to go tell people who had been standing in line later in the day that we had sold out. I was astonished at how friendly and understanding they were about not getting to have any food from us. Don't ever let them tell you New Yorkers aren't nice. We served brisket sliders with Apple-Jicama Chipotle Slaw. It's something our friend and consulting chef Jim Tripi worked up for us and it was a huge hit. You can do the same at home. Just put a little sliced or chopped brisket on a slider bun with a bit of barbecue sauce and add this slaw.

We always love an opportunity to share the Salt Lick with people outside of the state. There's nothing more exciting than having a full line of folks in New York City waiting to have a little taste of Texas.

1½ pounds jicama, julienned

2 pounds cabbage, finely shredded

1½ pounds carrots, finely shredded

1½ pounds apples (Fuji), julienned

4 Anaheim chiles or other mild chiles, finely diced

2 bunches cilantro

3 scallions, bias cut

½ cup sliced garlic

½ cup apple cider vinegar

¼ cup honey

½ cup sugar

½ cup orange juice

½ cup sugar

2 tablespoons avocado oil or high quality olive oil

Salt and pepper to taste

5 fresh jalapeños, thinly sliced

Combine all ingredients and adjust seasoning, adding jalapeños depending on heat desired.

FIRE-ROASTED TOMATOES WITH
GOAT CHEESE AND PARSLEY PESTO

THIS IS ONE of our most popular appetizers at catering events. Pear tomatoes work best for fire roasting. They are delicate but have a lot of flavor and sweetness that works well with the smokiness of the fire.

2 cups chopped flat-leaf parsley leaves
2 tablespoons toasted pine nuts
1 ½ tablespoons grated fresh Parmigiano-Reggiano cheese
1 teaspoon extra virgin olive oil
¼ teaspoon salt

For the pesto, combine all ingredients in food processor until smooth, and set aside.

16 yellow pear tomatoes
16 red pear tomatoes
Olive oil

Slice tomatoes in half lengthwise (from stem to tip) and brush cut sides with olive oil. Place cut-side down over medium flame on gas grill. If using charcoal grill, place tomatoes in middle of grill over briquettes that are medium hot (the briquettes should be completely covered in ash, and you should be able to hold your hand a couple of inches above grill for about 5 seconds).

When tomatoes develop dark char marks (5 to 8 minutes, depending on size and heat), use tongs to flip over. Continue cooking until skins begin to blacken in spots. Then remove tomatoes from grill, pile in bowl, drizzle with a little parsley pesto, cover with plastic, and set aside.

1 baguette or ciabatta roll
4 ounces goat cheese, soft
Chopped flat-leaf parsley leaves for garnish

For the crostini, slice bread into ¼-inch slices. Lightly brush both sides with parsley pesto. Toast crostini over high heat on grill or in broiler. Be careful while toasting, as crostini can easily burn. They need only 1 or 2 minutes per side on grill.

Once crostini are toasted, spread each with light amount of goat cheese, top with 2 tomatoes, and drizzle with parsley pesto. Garnish with chopped parsley.

SMOKED PORK PORTERHOUSE WITH
ORANGE BLOSSOM HONEY–SAGE CREAM SAUCE

COLD SMOKING is a technique we like to use to get smoke flavor into meats that we intend to prepare a different way, that is, on the grill. The temperature for cold smoking should remain under 100 degrees. At that temperature, foods take on a smoke flavor but remain relatively moist. In this case, you're not after heat. You're simply after smoke, so you need to place your meat as far away from the heat source as possible. Once you've done that, you have only about 4 hours to cook the meat on the grill (or in the oven). Otherwise, you need to immediately get the temperature of the meat below 38 degrees to maintain meat safety. The smoking time will vary per item and by size. It takes a little more finesse to master cold smoking, but it's well worth the effort. This dish is great with Hatch Macaroni and Four Cheeses, a recipe my friend Jim Tripi, executive chef at the Spanish Oaks Golf Course, created for us.

Always have your grill fired up and ready to go so that you can begin cooking your pork once the cold smoking process is finished.

Pork Porterhouse:
4 pork porterhouse steaks
1 tablespoon garlic salt and 1 teaspoon white pepper, combined

Place pork in cold smoker at 90 degrees, keeping it as far from heat source as possible. After 1 hour, remove and refrigerate. When time to serve, season meat and grill to desired doneness over live oak coals, if possible (charcoal fire will do).

Orange Blossom Honey–Sage Cream Sauce:
2 tablespoons butter (unsalted)
1 large sage leaf
1 cup half-and-half
2 tablespoons Wondra flour
¼ teaspoon salt
⅛ teaspoon pepper
1½ teaspoons orange blossom honey
1 teaspoon orange juice
¼ teaspoon orange zest
¼ teaspoon lime juice

In cast-iron skillet, melt butter over low heat. Add sage leaf and cook for 5 minutes to incorporate the flavor. Remove leaf and discard. In small cup, mix some of the half-and-half with flour until smooth (no lumps). Add mixture to remaining half-and-half, and mix well. Add salt, pepper, and honey, and stir until mixed. Place mixture into skillet with flavored butter, and bring to a boil over medium heat, stirring constantly. Boil 1 minute and remove from heat.

HATCH MACARONI AND FOUR CHEESES

3 gallons salted water
3 pounds cavatappi pasta or other pasta
½ pound butter
2 cups minced 1015 onions
½ pound flour
1 quart whole milk, warmed
1 quart heavy whipping cream
1 pound local cheddar
1 pound shredded mozzarella
1 cup shredded Parmesan
2 tablespoons fresh thyme leaves
¼ cup minced fresh chives
½ cup blended chipotle in adobo sauce
¼ cup minced fresh garlic
4 cups diced roasted, skinned, and seeded Hatch chiles
3 cups medium diced crispy smoky bacon or smoked pork rib meat, optional
1 cup goat cheese
Salt and pepper to taste

Bring water to boil, cook pasta until al dente, cool, and set aside. Heat butter in heavy-bottom pan, add onions, and saute until translucent. Add flour, and cook roux 10 to 15 minutes over low heat. Add milk and cream, stirring to prevent lumps, and bring mixture to slight boil. Add cheddar and mozzarella, and continue stirring until smooth, 4 to 5 minutes. Add Parmesan followed by herbs, spices, chiles, and optional meat. Remove from heat, and blend in goat cheese. Season to taste.

Crumb topping:
1 cup melted butter
5 cups Panko breadcrumbs
1 tablespoon garlic salt
1 tablespoon smoked paprika
1 tablespoon onion powder
1 tablespoon ground black pepper
5 cups shredded cheddar

Preheat oven to 350 degrees. Add butter to breadcrumbs and spices in bowl, and combine well. Add cheddar, and mix until blended through. Pour cheese mixture over pasta and stir to coat. Place pasta mixture in individual casserole dishes or large baking dish. Top with crumb mixture, and bake 10 minutes, until golden brown and delicious.

SMOKED CURRIED OYSTER ON
SWEET POTATO CHIP WITH CUCUMBER SAUCE

ON ONE OF our first forays into commercial cooking outside of barbecue, one of our clients had asked for an appetizer that used Texas Gulf oysters. We made them, but since we're all about smoking our meat, of course we had to smoke them too.

Smoked Curried Oyster:
16 oysters
1 tablespoon curry powder
1 tablespoon all-purpose flour
Pinch salt
3 tablespoons vegetable oil

Sweet Potato Chip:
Vegetable oil, for frying
2 large sweet potatoes, washed and sliced into ¼-inch disks
Salt Lick Dry Rub, see page 183, or sugar to taste

Cucumber Sauce:
1 medium cucumber, peeled, seeded, and finely chopped
½ teaspoon salt
8 ounces plain nonfat yogurt
1 clove garlic, crushed
1 tablespoon chopped chives or scallion

This is a burst of flavor in just one bite. We love to use Gulf oysters when we can. For a different spin on the chip, try yucca instead of sweet potato.

For the smoked curried oysters: Place raw oysters on a sheet pan. Place sheet pan away from the heat source in a 90-degree smoker for 20 to 30 minutes, until they have absorbed the smoke flavor. Remove for later use. Whisk together curry powder, flour, and salt in shallow bowl. Dredge oysters in mixture one at a time, shaking off excess flour, and transfer to plate. Heat oil in 10-inch heavy skillet until hot but not smoking, and pan fry oysters in batches, turning once until slightly crisp on the outside, 1 to 2 minutes. Transfer oysters to paper towels to drain.

For the sweet potato chip: In large saucepan, heat oil to 350 degrees. Fry potatoes 1½ to 3 minutes, stirring frequently. Remove from oil and drain on paper towel. Sprinkle with Salt Lick Dry Rub.

For the cucumber sauce: Place cucumber into strainer, sprinkle with salt, and let stand 15 minutes. Press out liquid with back of spoon to drain. Place in food processor with remaining ingredients, and blend well. Refrigerate until ready to serve. Makes 1 cup.

To serve, place oysters on chips. Spoon scant tablespoon cucumber sauce onto each oyster.

We begin harvesting our grapes in late summer, assuming the season has gone well. Everything is hand picked and sent to a winery to be pressed and made into beautiful Texas wine.

KATHARINE MAILE ROBERTS

Katharine Maile Roberts

Bᴇᴄᴀᴜsᴇ ᴏꜰ ᴍʏ ᴡɪꜰᴇ's medical challenges, doctors told us that we would never have children. But sometimes life has other plans. We found out early one fall that we were pregnant. When my wife's doctor found out, he came unglued. He screamed at both of us for a while before finally calming down. Despite his greatest concerns, we welcomed Katharine Maile Roberts on May 25, 1984. She was our own little miracle. Her mother named her "Maile" after a popular Hawaiian flowering vine used to make leis. She was a sweet, gentle baby who rarely ever cried.

As she grew up, we found she had a quiet nature but a strong spirit. She was constantly finding ways to challenge herself. When she was 12, she attended a Catholic boarding school in Austin. She told us she was bored, needed a challenge, and had decided to go to a boarding school in Hawaii. She had researched the school, had applied, and was accepted before we knew it. Though it was hard to let her go, we were proud of her for wanting to test her independence. We took her there and toured around the area where she would live. While we were unpacking in her new room, she sat down on her bed with tears streaming down her face. I asked her, "Maile, what on earth is wrong?" She gave me an earnest look and said, "Pappa, I think the enormity of what I've done has just dawned on me."

I reassured her that she had made a good decision. My wife, Susan, and I stayed in a nearby hotel for a few days as she settled in. The next morning, the headmaster of the school called and said we had to come get her. She was distraught and wanted to go home. I took her for a walk. I explained to her that she could come home right then and there if she wanted to. I added that she should remember how proud everyone was of her and that a lot of her family looked up to her for being so strong. I told her she owed it to herself to give it a chance. Then I said, "Listen, if you stick it out and make good grades, when you're 16, I'll buy you a car." I waited a few seconds before I added, "Just don't tell your mother." She nodded in agreement, and we walked back to the room, where Susan was waiting for us.

The second we opened the door, Maile announced to Susan that I promised to buy her a car. (I never made that mistake again.) We intended to stay three or four days while she settled in. The first couple of days she called at 7 in the morning and then after dinner and before bedtime. But as the days passed, the calls slowed. We went to visit her one day, and when she saw us she said, "I thought you guys had already gone home."

That's when we knew she was doing okay and we could leave. Six years later, she graduated and continued her independent streak by going to Emory University. It wasn't until she graduated that she came back home to Austin to get her MBA at the University of Texas.

In 2010 I got a call from Brian Loring, the young man she had dated since college. He asked if he could stop by to visit with Susan and me. He then sat us down and told us that he wanted to marry Maile. We knew this day was coming. After all, the two had been inseparable. But we were still stunned. I don't think a parent—especially a father—is ever ready to give his daughter away. While it's tradition for a man to ask a father for his daughter's hand, I didn't feel it was a request that involved just me. I asked Brian to let Susan and me talk it over in private. Out of respect for Susan, it was important that we both decided whether to give Brian our blessing. Giving her that respect was one of the wisest decisions I've made in our marriage.

After we had talked it over, I said to Brian, "Don't think we're not excited. We've just never had this happen before, and you're never quite ready." We both gave him our approval and told him we were thrilled for them.

He then asked if we could help him organize the proposal. He knew how much Maile loved the vineyards we had planted at the Salt Lick. He wanted to propose to her there, but he needed our help to make it a special surprise. He had everything planned to the last detail. He wanted to propose at a certain spot in the vineyard and then walk to the stone house near one of the ponds and have a special dinner. We helped him organize a photographer and a makeshift kitchen at the stone house and had a chef prepare the meal.

As a rather meticulous planner, Brian even had a Plan B, just in case it rained. I kidded with him one evening on the phone: "What about Plan C?" He seemed confused and asked why he would need a third plan. I responded, "What if she says no?" He wasn't too fond of the thought. I had to reassure him that I was just pulling his leg.

That is how I knew he was the right guy for Maile. Any man who will go to great lengths to bring a smile to your daughter's face is a good candidate to be her husband. (Plus, he's a man who works hard and has good character, and it doesn't hurt that he has also passed the bar exam, has an MBA from the University of Texas, and, best of all, has a job.) His explanation to Maile for going to the vineyards was that he needed some photos for a marketing project for one of his graduate classes. Once he got her to just the right spot, he knelt on one knee and popped the question. He did allow us a few minutes to hide behind the stone house until she said yes. After that, we gave them

This is the first wedding we've ever performed in our vineyards. I think our 2011 wines will be a good vintage.

both big hugs and left them to enjoy their evening.

Weeks later she came to me and asked if she could host her wedding in the vineyards. At the time, I thought we might have some problems, considering there was no structure to host a big wedding there. But when you get creative and have a creative staff to help you execute, anything is possible. What began as plans for a small wedding soon transformed into a project of epic proportions. We devised a large frame for a 10,000-square-foot temporary pavilion beside the vineyards. We added glass-panel walls for the dinner reception and a pathway through the vines down to the original engagement spot to host the wedding ceremony. As with all wedding planning, there were highs and lows, both with logistics and with emotions, but on October 22, 2011, Maile and Brian held a beautiful wedding, beginning their life together, in the same area where her family began their lives more than 100 years before.

My daughter comes from a line of strong, determined women. My great grandmother crossed hundreds of miles to get to this part of Texas. She planted our roots here and raised a family along the way. My grandmother, Roxie, was the glue for our place in Driftwood. She set her own path through marriage, raised a family, managed a farm, forged deep, longstanding friendships within the community, and guided my perspective on life when I was growing up. My mother left her home and heritage in Hawaii to begin a new life Texas. She supported my father in his endeavors but never lost who she was. Her work ethic and resourcefulness are the two characteristics that crafted the foundation for the Salt Lick. And among the many things my wife, Susan, has brought to this family, the most inspiring are her strength and will to live.

I had a dream once that Maile was on a large stage to receive a great award. It was many years in the future. She was old and walked with a wooden cane. She wore a pretty white dress and colorful leis draped around her neck. There were thousands of people there in all sorts of colors. They were all related to her and her family somehow, and they were all there to celebrate a special award for her. In the front row were the women of my family. Bettie, Roxie, Hisako, Susan, and aunts and cousins as well. It was as if everyone was there to show how proud they were of who she had become. It was a powerful dream to me because I realized then that most of the stories you read in the history of Texas, or any history for that matter, are about the men who played key roles in bringing about change. But, in truth, this story is more about strong Texas women than about strong Texas men. Without women like Bettie, Roxie, Hisako, and Susan, there would be no Driftwood, at least not like it is today. The dream made me realize that this is not my story; I'm just the messenger. Maile is the next chapter to this story. And I look forward to seeing what her strength and tenacity will reveal.

A Perfect Wedding Recipe

Combine family and friends with one of the most wonderful daughters any parent could wish for and a smart, hardworking young man who loves her as much as she loves him. Place them in a beautiful vineyard on her family's land of more than 100 years, and you have the recipe for one of the best wedding celebrations a father could give to his little girl. May their journey be exceptionally splendid!

Susan and I had no idea we'd be giving our daughter away in the middle of our vineyards, but on a warm autumn evening in October 2011, we did exactly that, underneath the Texas skies and surrounded by family and friends.

NEW POTATOES WITH ROSEMARY

WHEN IT WASN'T mashed potatoes, my grandmother, Roxie, would make new potatoes. Though I don't have her exact recipe, I played with a version of it a few years back, using decorative rosemary I had in the front yard. I rolled the potatoes in olive oil, garlic salt, and white pepper, like she did. But then I made a bed of rosemary on the bottom of an iron skillet, put the potatoes on top, and roasted them the oven. I made them once for my wife and daughter, and I'll never forget it as the very first time Maile said she liked my cooking. That's when I knew I had made it as a cook.

2 pounds new potatoes, whole*
3 tablespoons olive oil
Garlic salt and white pepper to taste
4 to 5 sprigs rosemary
You can also use small purple potatoes or Yukon gold potatoes, cut in 1-inch chunks.

Heat oven to 350 degrees. Roll potatoes in olive oil to create a light coating and season liberally. Rub sprigs of rosemary in olive oil to prevent burning and lay them along skillet bottom. Place potatoes on rosemary, and roast for 40 minutes or until potatoes are soft on the inside and crisp on the outside. Serves 4 to 5.

SONORAN DRY RUB

THIS IS A recipe Maile got from a friend from the West Texas town of Sonora. The spices in this rub have a distinct Mexican influence. This is a go-to rub for just about any meat for grilling, including chicken, pork, and beef, and is good for fish too. Combine a batch, and keep it on hand while you're cooking.

1 tablespoon black pepper
1 tablespoon salt
2 teaspoons cayenne pepper
1 teaspoon granulated garlic
1 teaspoon chili dulce
1 teaspoon paprika

MAILE'S GRILLED CHEESE BRISKET SANDWICH

THIS IS A sandwich Maile came up with that is just delicious. She really wanted us to serve this sandwich in our short-lived Austin food trailer, but we decided not to. In the end, the trailer wasn't very successful. It may just be because we didn't put this sandwich on the menu. *NOTE: Add any level of condiments to suit your tastes, but out of respect for Maile, please avoid pickles. That's the one thing she just can't stand—even if they're on the same table. So please, no pickles.*

2 to 3 tablespoons olive oil
Kosher salt and fresh cracked pepper
1 to 2 tablespoons Salt Lick Original Recipe Bar-B-Que Sauce
4 slices rustic sourdough bread
1 cup mild semi-firm goat cheese, grated on large holes of box grater
½ pound sliced or chopped brisket
Arugula or watercress

Heat a 12-inch skillet on medium. Drizzle olive oil in pan, and add a dash of kosher salt and 1 to 2 cracks of fresh pepper. Spread barbecue sauce on bread slices. Sprinkle half the cheese over two slices. Place half the brisket on top of the cheese. Add greens and top with the remaining cheese. Top each with a bread slice, pressing down gently to set.

Place sandwiches in skillet. Cook until crisp and deep golden brown, 5 to 10 minutes per side, flipping sandwiches back to first side to reheat and crisp, about 15 seconds. Watch sandwiches carefully, checking often to avoid scorching. Serve immediately. Serves 2.

Variation: You can use Lauren's Spicy Recipe Bar-B-Que Sauce if you like a sandwich with a little kick.

MAILE'S WEDDING FILET MIGNON

TO SAVE MY SANITY, Maile did not want Salt Lick food served at her wedding. Instead, she hired chef James Tripi, whom we knew as the executive chef for the Spanish Oaks Golf Resort in Austin. Though Chef Tripi had taken a position as the executive chef at Yellowstone Club in Montana shortly after the wedding proposal, we were lucky to get him to agree to serve at the wedding. By the time the date arrived, Tripi had moved back to his job at Spanish Oaks. Despite serving private parties for the likes of Justin Timberlake and Leonardo DiCaprio, Tripi decided Montana was just too cold for his blood. The highlights of the wedding meal included beef tenderloin and grilled sea bass.

Herb butter:
1½ sticks butter, room temperature
3 tablespoons chopped fresh chives
1½ tablespoons chopped fresh tarragon
1 small garlic clove, pressed

Mix ingredients in small bowl for herb butter. Season to taste.

6 1-inch-thick filet mignons
Salt and pepper

Sprinkle steaks with salt and pepper. Melt 2 tablespoons herb butter in heavy large nonstick skillet over medium heat. Add steaks to skillet, and cook to desired doneness, about 6 minutes per side for medium rare. Transfer steaks to plates. Place 1 tablespoon herb butter atop each steak, let rest 5 to 10 minutes, and serve.

MAILE'S WEDDING SEA BASS

4 8-ounce fillets of sea bass, scaled, skin on
2 tablespoons extra virgin olive oil
Kosher salt and white pepper

Preheat oven to 400 degrees. Brush fillets with 1 tablespoon olive oil. Season with salt and pepper. Place medium sauté pan over high heat. Add remaining tablespoon olive oil, and sauté fish skin-side down for 2 minutes. Transfer to the oven and bake until done, 5 to 6 minutes. Do not turn the fish, to ensure a crispy skin.

The pressure was on to make the perfect steak for more than 400 people at Maile's wedding, but our saving grace is our exceptional staff, who rise to the challenge of every task we've put them to. You can't ask for anything better than that.

Maile Roberts – In Her Own Words

I DON'T THINK there was ever one particular moment when I decided I wanted to be involved with the Salt Lick restaurant business. I have just always known that's what I would do. I know my parents would support me in any career I choose, but for me, this seems like the next best step.

Although I was born in Austin (May 25, 1984), the restaurant is really a home to me. I grew up going there for all of my birthdays. When I was in elementary school, my mom would pack Salt Lick pork ribs in my lunch box. I got made fun of so many times that I eventually asked her to stop and pack me "normal" boring sandwich lunches.

I grew up headstrong, like a lot of members in my family, my mom, my dad, and my grandparents. I was always looking for new challenges. Although I would have been perfectly happy to go to middle and high school in Austin, I had heard about this great school in Hawaii, where my parents met. I told my parents about it, and they both agreed that if I applied and got in, they would let me go. I was only 12 years old, but at the time, it seemed like something I just had to do. It wasn't easy living away from home all that time, but somehow I knew I'd always be back. This was my chance to see other places and experience other things.

I'm a University of Texas Longhorn at heart, but having gone to such a small high school, I thought UT was just too big for me. So it came down to Washington and Lee University and Emory University. I ended up choosing Emory because Atlanta appealed to me as a larger metropolitan area as opposed to the more rural countryside of Lexington, Virginia.

And while I still had a heart for home, if I hadn't gone to Emory, I wouldn't have met Brian Loring, whom I married in October 2011. We started dating in 2005, and we both ended up coming to Austin to get our MBAs from UT. Now that I'm back home, I'm excited to get more involved in working with my family's business.

My goals for the business are simple, to keep doing what my family has been doing for more than 40 years: make great barbecue. But I want to see the Salt Lick grow. Right now it's a destination that people from all over the world visit. But I'd love to see it grow into other cities, not only in Texas but in other states. After living in Atlanta, I can now say that not every place has great barbecue. That's something I took for granted, growing up in a family barbecue business.

When I was still in college, my dad decided to plant vineyards and start making wine. I had no idea he'd pull off something like that, but as I've come into the circle, I see it is one of the best ideas he's ever had—and believe me, he has a lot of ideas. I've loved working with Salt Lick Cellars on creating its own brand. I helped design the wine labels and even the interior of the building. As time goes on, I see us playing a big role in the Texas wine industry, which is growing stronger every year.

But even though I want to see new things in the future of the Salt Lick, I think it's important to know about the foundation that made it so great. I worked as a waitress in the summertime with the staff and kitchen crew. Most people have no idea how much effort goes into operating a place as big as this. We have stations in the kitchen for workers specifically devoted to making sauce or coleslaw or potato salad so that it's always fresh all day, every day.

In the front of the house, so much is going on, especially on the weekends, when we are serving thousands of people. When I was a lot younger, I served drinks and desserts, but working as a waitress, I realized how hard a job it was. We've got a pretty small menu, but that doesn't really make things easier.

When people come in, they expect the food to be consistently great all the time. That's not easy to do. And when it's not just how the customer expects it to be, believe me, they will let you know. It takes a big team to work together to make sure everything comes out just right. That's something my grandfather and my father have worked hard to create all these years, and I'm looking forward to the challenge of carrying that on.

Before, I used to describe the Salt Lick to friends who had never heard of it as a great big barbecue place that feeds 800 people at once and lets you bring your own beer. Now I know it's so much more than that. It's a big family of people who work hard to serve other families a great time and great food. It's what being a Texan is all about.

The Salt Lick is an important place for me, so important that I held my wedding there. My husband proposed to me in my father's vineyards, and we got married just a few feet from that spot. Then we celebrated with friends, staff, and, most importantly, family in a place where my roots began more than 100 years ago.

About the Authors

SCOTT ROBERTS

SCOTT ROBERTS has spent his life fostering a family heritage that began in Driftwood, Texas, more than 100 years ago and building on a dream he and his parents began in 1967 with the Salt Lick barbecue restaurant. Many people say that when it comes to a great barbecue restaurant, the barbecue itself is what's most important, but to Roberts it's the smiles on his customers' faces that mean the most. "Remember," he says. "I am not a chef. Just a cook."

A WORD OF THANKS:
I opened this book thanking the strong Texas women in my life who have shaped who I am today. But there are a few others who helped make this book a reality, including Angela Hobbs, Silver Garza, George Jacquez, Miriam Wilson, and Jim and Maria Tripi. I'd also like to thank Jessica Dupuy for spending almost a year, driving out to the Salt Lick and finding a way to put my story into a book. My name may be on the cover, but she's the one who really wrote it.

JESSICA DUPUY

JESSICA DUPUY is a freelance writer who has written for *Texas Monthly, National Geographic Traveler, Imbibe, Texas Highways,* and numerous Austin and regional publications. She has also written *Uchi: The Cookbook,* in conjunction with James Beard Award–winning executive chef Tyson Cole. Dupuy lives in Austin with her husband, her two Duck Tolling retrievers, and her son, Gus. She enjoys cooking, traveling, triathlons, and fly-fishing, and she is a member of Les Dames D'Escoffier–Austin, Foodways Texas, and the Wine and Food Foundation of Texas.

A WORD OF THANKS TO:
Myers Dupuy for being my tireless editor, best friend, and constant support, I love you; Gus Dupuy for smiling every day; Janice Stewart and Jim and Martha Norman for always loving and supporting me; Tyson Cole for giving me my first chance with a cookbook; Julie Savasky, Kenny Braun, Angela Hobbs, George Jacquez, Silver Garza, Layne Lynch, Hannah Norman, and Dana Frank, without whose help this book would never have made it to press. Most importantly, thank you to Scott Roberts, who trusted me to write a book about the story of his life, his family, and his love for Driftwood.

INDEX